On Being Old

(with Acceptance and Gratitude)

Mary Jo MacIntyre

Nadine Ann Shirley

Sandra (Sam) Studiner

DORRANCE PUBLISHING CO
EST. 1920
PITTSBURGH, PENNSYLVANIA 15238

Dorrance Publishing Co
585 Alpha Drive
Suite 103
Pittsburgh, PA 15238
Visit our website at *www.dorrancebookstore.com*

ISBN: 979-8-88604-359-4
eISBN: 979-8-88604-452-2

For Our Loved Ones

Contents

Introduction

"Do not regret growing older. It's a privilege denied to many."

Author Unknown

This is a true story of how three friends happened to get together after many years of total separation from each other. We had so much in common when we first met, including children. One of us had four children, one had five, and one had six. The more powerful common denominator at the time, however, was not the kids but the Catholic Church and an offshoot thereof called a Cursillo. We had a few short years of bonding to build a real foundation for our friendships, and then as life and family took precedence we lost contact with each other. One moved with her family out of state, another divorced and went back into the working world, and the third became totally ensconced in her active family.

It was a funeral forty years later (FORTY YEARS) that sparked a reunion. Sam and Nadine ran into each other at that funeral, after which Sam called Mary Jo and a long overdue lunch meeting followed. As will be no surprise to anyone who has had very good friends there was not one instance of hesitance, discomfort or tension. We took up right where we left off, talking and laughing, questioning and filling each other in about our lives. Of course we talked about husbands and children, grandchildren and great-grandchildren, mutual friends and the general path each of our lives had taken. We also discussed the feelings that come with aging, the fears, and the physical changes. There were actual belly laughs over our shared bowel issues. We communicated more honestly now than in our younger days and covered topics that we had not in the past. There was no more competition or trying to impress, just the need to talk about anything and everything with another person of our own age who we knew would understand.

So just how old are we? Sam, whose given name is Sandra but prefers her nickname, is the youngest at age 75. She is still married to her original husband after 56 years, has 5 adult children, 16 grandchildren and 3 great-grandchildren, all living within 120 miles of her. She is a tall, formerly brunette now graying, senior. She has her feet solidly on the ground with a practical approach to life. She is physically active herself and has a love of all sports, with an emphasis on baseball. In addition she is very creative and self-aware.

Nadine is next at age 79. She was divorced after 30 years of marriage and has now been single for as long as she was married. She has 6 adult children, 9 grandchildren, and 3 greats. She has moved back to her home state of Montana after having been gone 30+ years and has only one child close by. The other five are in three different states. She was a brunette in the distant past who has recently let her hair turn to its natural white. She is first and foremost big on thinking and communicating with sensitivity and empathy for others. She has a fundamental connection to the mysteries of life and what makes people tick.

Mary Jo is the oldest of this group at age 81 with beautiful white hair. She was divorced after 26 years of marriage and has now been single for 32 years. She has 4 adult children, 11 grandchildren and 3 greats. Her children are all local with the exception of her eldest daughter, who lives with her family in Ireland, giving Mary Jo the incentive to travel there as often as she can manage. She has a predominantly emotional approach to life with a strong emphasis on nurturing. She has the ability to take charge and even shows a little temper now and then.

All of us have been physically healthy well into our seventies with only minor ailments to date. We are all intelligent, mentally curious and are still mentally sharp, most of the time. (LOL) Two of us struggled financially for many years, but at this stage of life we are all comfortable. We were all reared in protestant homes (two Methodist and one Episcopalian) and joined the Catholic Church when marrying Catholic men. Two of us remain Catholic with the third identifying as a Christian but not Catholic. Two of us were pregnant when we got married. Yes, it happened in the good old days too, one resulting in a set of fraternal twins. We were all married when all our children were born, which might seem a bit old-fashioned today. Emotionally we have all weathered many storms, some ending with lessons learned and appreciated and some leaving us with regrets.

By the end of that first meeting we all decided that we needed to do this more often so agreed to meet monthly. Interestingly enough each of us was very much looking forward to the second meeting, to the extent that Sam had actually made a list of the issues she wanted to bring up. She was concerned about the fact that Nadine had indicated feeling low with no discernable reason or even ability to verbalize the actual feelings.

All three of us were aware that there was a space in our lives that these get-togethers filled. For Nadine it was the ability to talk about anything she had on her mind and know that it would be received respectfully. For Mary Jo it was the ability to have in-depth discussions on many subjects that as a younger woman she never talked about. And for Sam it fulfilled her need for a more solid friendship base and hoped that it would provide the same to the others.

By our third meeting the idea was introduced to actually put on paper the essence of our discussions. We had already determined that our sharing of life experiences into old age was beneficial to each of us, so perhaps it would be to others also. That is our fondest wish for putting in book form a compilation of those discussions. Enjoy!

Chapter One
Physical Health, Medicine and Body Parts

"I don't mind getting older but my body is taking it badly."

Crazy Mama,
from *Journal, Her Life and Kids*

It seems perfectly logical that our first chapter would be about the physical body and the changes that occur with the aging process. People start talking about those changes in their 60s, 50s and even 40s. Strangers talk to each other about their aches and pains and body limitations that weren't there a few years ago. We are no different. Since I am the nurse in this threesome, I, Mary Jo, am the presenter of Chapter One on bodies that got old.

So first up is Sam's look at what generally happens as we age, and it makes her wonder why our mothers didn't tell us, warn us, or prepare us about growing old so that we wouldn't have to be so surprised by the process. At any rate one of the reasons we decided to write our stories is that maybe we can give some of our readers a "heads up." Sam says, "I was quite surprised to see my first signs of aging when I was 35 years old. REALLY?!?! A gray hair already?" First signs, besides gray hair, most people begin to see a fluctuation in their weight. Energy level follows that. So much of those two happenings stem from our jobs/careers and lifestyles. We then move into the health issues that require doctoring and medicines. Some people say those medicines could be part of the problems we encounter. Too many pills, too many combinations, incorrect prescriptions, and the cost of the ones we need but can't afford to get.

Now we get on with the midlife, age-appropriate, malfunctions of our bodies and proceed to where we have ended up today—OLD! From head to toe we experience the age-old process of old-age. Sam says, "Let's start at the top!" Hair begins to thin and/or fall out. Stress, worry, medications (again!) and any number of things can be responsible. Hearing lessens. It seems men are more susceptible, but women are holding their own in that department. And, loose crystals IN the ears are not the same as crystals ON the ears! Eyes weaken and cataracts become a necessary surgery. Noses and ears, they say, keep growing throughout life. Ugh!! But so do the problems with sinuses, nasal drip, smelling and not smelling. Teeth, sometimes more often than not, need to be replaced, capped, filled, and cleaned, even if you were a staunch brusher and flosser. "Long in the tooth" has deeper meaning! We haven't even mentioned what happens to our face due to lines, drooping skin and baggy eyes. Nor have we acknowledged the mental capacity of our brains as we age, including dementia and its family of illnesses.

Sam continues, moving on down (and that is no pun!) we get to deal with a turkey neck, sagging boobs, no-strength arms, arthritic hands, and a back that never learned to lift things correctly. Inside this wonderful region of the human body we have a heart that has sustained us for better than three quarters of a century but once in a while tries to rebel with any number of things, yet keeps right on beating—a miracle in itself! As women with children we've watched our tummies expand and contract with each childbirth and never really return to its original form. Because of THIS miracle our urinary tracts and vaginas (a word never mentioned in our generation) become affected in ways no one told us to expect. Depends, or adult diapers, become normal conversational words. I won't even go into the IBS (irritable bowel syndrome). Sam says she can't believe there are doctors willing to specialize in that area, but thank God there are!

Now, if you've spent any time on your feet, we're looking at hip and knee replacement. And those two surgeries are on the assembly line these days. All of this descending aging process ultimately ends up going south and the only thing left to catch it is our feet, hence neuropathy, planters fasciitis, bunions, and the inability to cut our own toenails, let alone dance like we once did. "The largest organ of the human body is our skin, and as we age, it becomes a breeding ground for unknown and unwanted growths that don't feel or look like they belong there, including extraneous facial hairs."

Sam adds, "If, when we were young, we knew all this would happen we might have said, 'Shoot me now.' But our saving grace is that everyone goes through some, or all of it, and there is comfort in numbers, in our case, our friends. Getting old, as they say, is not for sissies. Had we known we would end up like this would we have taken better care of ourselves? Probably not. It is a typical, unconscious mindset when we were young to think we would 'live forever,' (if we even thought about it at all), hopefully remaining healthy during the course of our remaining years. Being a dancer, athlete, gymnast, skater, and mother of five probably contributed to the overall decline of my body. But in retrospect those years were so memorable and fun that I should never complain about the results they incurred. Not until I was in my thirties did I realize that I was aging and needed to be cognizant of my body and what was needed for preservation. Now I'm dealing with the results. The secret is to do whatever you can without wallowing or whining, unless our friends allow it, keep putting one foot in front of the other, and be glad you're on this side of the green grass for now! My most tolerant internist whom I told many years ago that I expected her to keep me alive for as long as possible, has been very kind and patient in referring me to whatever specialist can solve my ongoing complaints. I believe if something isn't right, get it fixed! As a result of many doctors' office visits, I have copied a running list of all of my procedures and medications to hand in to admittance so that I don't have to test my memory when filling out their forms."

"So, after seventy-five years, I am still hanging in there, wanting to keep going and making the best of what time I have left. I once told an old friend of mine at a high school reunion that I never considered myself pretty, but I worked very hard at being presentable. The Covid-19 pandemic and its isolation requirements have even taken THAT out of the equation since the daily attire consists of sweats and no makeup," Sam concludes.

According to Nadine, the statement she has made several times to several people is, "I have aged more in the last 2 years than I have in the past 20 years," definitely in reference to her physical body. She's not sure when she actually started noticing the rapid changes, but she had to have a total hip replacement in October of last year and, although the surgery was successful and her recovery has been normal, she doesn't feel anywhere near as capable as she was previously. "Just this past week I spent four days with my eldest daughter, visiting from California, trying to be helpful in our attempt to do some cleaning in our cabin. I assumed the minor job of wiping out the kitchen cabinets and placing shelf lining therein. Very quickly it became obvious that I could not reach the high shelves, because I couldn't stand on the top step of the small ladder, and I could not reach the bottom shelves, because I couldn't bend deeply enough. In addition, I did not have enough strength to put bed skirts on the beds or carry most supplies in from the car." Her daughter is 60 years old and she could do all of that easily.

Her first awareness of the decline in physical ability was when she was in her late 50s. She had decided to go back to school and was working toward a Master's Degree in Social Work. The administration had brought in a Ropes Course which is for team building awareness. She was one of two who sat out the entire day. The realization that her body did not have the strength and/or stamina to perform on the various forms of apparatus was surprising and left her with a sense of insecurity. Another experience along the same lines, but even more startling, was when she slipped one of the Richard Simmons *Sweatin' to the Oldies* discs into the player with the intent of dancing around her living room all by herself. "Yikes! I could not move my feet fast enough. Having been a relatively good dancer, I was both shocked and very disappointed, to say the least."

A sometimes humorous, but always fascinating exercise for Nadine, is that of completing the health evaluation form in doctors' offices. She remembers the days when this meant answering "no" to item after item all the way to the end of the however many pages, excluding pregnancies (8) and live births (6). Now there are "yes" responses for all of the following: skin issues (vitiligo and eczema), eye problems (macular degeneration), acid reflux, heart problems (actually arterial something or other), bowel problems (maybe irritable bowel disorder), low thyroid, diabetes, arthritis, high blood pressure, and high cholesterol. Surgeries include a hysterectomy plus appendix removal at age 29, gall bladder at 48ish, cataracts (both eyes), bunion, and skin cancers on hand, arm and head, and now hip replacement, all in the 70s. "Oh, yes, I have had shingles three times also," she interjects.

Around age 30 she started taking thyroid pills, and that was her only prescription medication until about age 60 when a blood pressure medication was added. She is now on prescribed medications for thyroid, two for high blood pressure, acid reflux, diabetes, water retention, and high cholesterol. Add to those a list of over-the-counter medications for eyes, joints and allergies, plus vitamins and minerals a plenty. "My doctor's theory is that one prescribed medication for each decade of life is still okay, so I'm happy. I'm at 6 when it could be 8."

"I really have no right to complain, because as old bodies go, mine is doing very well, but I still find it discouraging. Having been used to a strong, healthy, dependable body and being reduced to limited strength, stamina and dexterity accompanied by increased, but still tolerable, pain has not been an easy adjustment. This might be the most unacceptable part of the aging process for me," concludes Nadine.

And now it's my turn; this is Mary Jo again. Just seeing the title of this chapter made me chuckle. Body parts! Aging! Not me. Everyone else does it but it is a state of mind. Right? Those damn body parts scream otherwise. There is no point in elaborating on each part since it is a common history. So just to be a bit more explicit, which one goes first? It all came on so fast, or at least, got my attention. The eyes got foggy, the bowls got lazy, the back now aches, the knees are going (and I have since this writing had my right knee replaced), while others complain of hips. Let's face it, the body wears out with time. So when it comes to elective surgeries, it all depends on how much pain you will tolerate. Cataract surgery and replacing joints kind of heads the list since both are pretty important to maintain independence. And at my age, independence is high on my list of priorities. As a divorced woman in my eighties, I am alone, and while that has its own rewards, it is a liability as the body gives out. Once I got through the denial (or was forced to) I realized that it helps to get the necessary surgeries while I still can. It happens when you finally arrive at the point of "forget fashion" and look for comfort and support. I do admire the women who continue to shop for the latest fashions, stay well groomed, nails done, and hair appointments on a regular basis. That used to be me. What got me to this stage?

It started with allergies and rashes. Then it followed with a kidney stone, a most painful experience. Then came jarring the back with a step down that I didn't see. It pinched the sciatic nerve and was the beginning of a two year battle with pain. The meds given caused hallucinations and a foggy brain which resulted in two falls. The last one did damage to my right arm and leg and resulted in a stay at a rehab center. In time, the mind cleared and the therapy went much better once I could cooperate. When I got home, the pain continued to grow more severe. Back into the hospital where it was discovered that there was an infection in my spine which was destroying discs and starting on a vertebrae. Back into rehab for another 4 weeks of

IV therapy. Once the infection was cleared up, a spinal fusion followed. At long last, I was pain free, and able to walk freely and back to being independent.

Let's face it, we all think we are stronger than the other guy. As a nurse, I was very guilty of that. It is hard to come to terms with your own vulnerability. The hardest part of aging is accepting it as truth. You are old. You now hear things like, "It is so fun to tease old ladies," or "You remind me so much of my grandma." I am a grandmother, in fact, a great grandmother, but it is hard to hear when you are in a social setting. Just for a short while, you forget that you aren't that fun, young person you once were.

I remember taking care of my father during his last years. He came from a small town where he was well known, liked, respected, and a mentor to many young men. He came to live with me as his health was failing. I saw how people treated him. They didn't know him so he was just an old man. It was hard for him and for me to see. Dignity and respect are important no matter what age!

What I am learning from all these experiences is to be grateful for life, for family, for friends, for the simple abilities to see, to work, to laugh, to eat, to move with limited pain and to accept the limitations that come with age. Celebrate life no matter the age we happen to be.

As a nurse in a doctor's office (an internist) about 70% of the patients were geriatric. The goal was not to reverse the irreversible aging process, but to make people more comfortable by managing their pains or healing any infections they may have or addressing any problems that can be resolved by surgery. If necessary, patients were referred to appropriate doctors. That pretty much summarizes my attitude for myself now. I do hope to remain healthy enough to stay independent and to reduce the aches and pains that come with aging. It helps a great deal to share these last years with friends who understand my limitations.

Chapter Two
Mental and Emotional Wellbeing

"Mental health is not a destination, but a process. It's about how you drive, not where you're going."

Noam Shpancer, Ph.D.

It also seems perfectly logical that mental and emotional wellbeing would follow physical as our Chapter 2. Haven't those designations for parts of a human being always gone together in your mind, i.e., physical, mental, and emotional? And just as logical is it that I, Nadine, as the Clinical Social Worker of the group, would be the presenter.

Let's start with what Mary Jo has to say on this topic. Since, according to her, she is pretty much ruled by emotions, her mental state does vacillate a bit. Circumstances in her life have left her with hopelessness, acceptance, depression (a lack of hope, not clinical depression), joy, and happiness. She sees herself as working through the tough times, knowing that time is essential to healing, then giving herself permission to be happy and to move on. This is in reference to her marriage and ultimate divorce. Her whole identity was in being a wife and mother. It took years for her to accept that it was okay to be single. She says, "Motherhood lasts a lifetime, thank you, Lord." When she was so weary, confused, and unable to get herself on solid ground, she sought help in a group called "Homes for Growth" in Canada. According to her, "Two weeks of soul searching and guidance was a big help!"

Mary Jo's life continued on an active basis in spite of her depression. She felt that getting out of the house and facing life and people was good medicine. Luckily, she had good friends that walked with her and encouraged her. One even gave Mary Jo a position as a nurse in her organization which opened new doors for her. It was okay to start with small jobs and one led to another, stepping stones in the work place and in life.

She even dated a few times. One was a friend from her college days. He was going through his own crisis and they found solace in each other. "It was that 'in love' feeling and a new one for both of us. I often told him that if ever I would write a biography, he would be my favorite chapter," laughs Mary Jo. He lived a long way away. So they rarely saw one another. They talked on the phone daily. He felt he couldn't leave his children and she felt the same about hers. "My husband had abandoned even his children, and I simply couldn't leave them to go to another state. Through tears we agreed to end it. It was a healing time for us both," she stated. "That need to be accepted, to be loved, is good for the soul. The road to happiness and healing is paved with the friends and people who dare to love you as you are—no strings, no expectations, just fun to be with! Laughter was our greatest gift to one another."

"It was friends and work and, above all, my children and grandchildren that filled my life and gave me purpose," she adds with obvious enthusiasm. The hole in her heart was filled with the love of others. As she gets older and faces physical limitations, she feels that the greatest gift given is to laugh with friends. She tends to enjoy the life she is given now, to see humor rather than judgment in so many actions (hers and others). She states, "It is healthy to surround yourself with friends who enjoy life and have fun living it with others. Once you focus on the positive in your life, acceptance is there. It, too, is a gift."

Sam is ready to join in. "Boy! What a roller-coaster life is for me in the mental and emotional wellbeing arena," she says. The one thing she learned through all the years of ups and downs is that if you just wait a day or two, things will change. (I, Nadine, need to interject at this point that my mother's favorite saying was, "This, too, shall pass.") However, not everyone learns to wait. They are the ones who suffer so much that they can only see release or peace through dramatic or life-threatening actions. She admitted to being there, several times. "The emotional suffering that people and circumstances present to us is in direct proportion to how much we can handle and when that jar gets filled something has got to happen," she says.

Sam said she was fortunate enough to have friends who allowed her to unload and confide in them when things got rough. One traumatic breakthrough came when she called her favorite priest for answers and he told her that she was accepting all the responsibility for something that wasn't her fault. True or not, a weight was lifted off her that day and set her free so she could begin to act instead of react to things that presented a stressful situation. "But what was it about me that I had spent years thinking everything was my fault? How vain and self-centered is that?" thought Sam. "Because I couldn't make things right, was I making them worse?"

Sam says she grew up in the make-believe world of television shows like *Donna Reed*, *Father Knows Best*, and *Leave It to Beaver*. Families were perfect on those shows. Their problems were all solved in one hour and everyone loved everyone else and got along, with lessons learned. Sam wanted her life to be like that! The more she wanted it the worse things got. "And I lost myself in the process," she said. Sometimes in marriage we become less of who we are in order to please our spouses. The trouble starts when we don't allow our spouses to be themselves. You don't live with the same person for 57 years and expect smooth sailing all the time.

According to Sam, making oneself mentally and emotionally well sometimes takes a traumatic turn and we have to choose if we're going to go down the healthy, happy road or the depressive, despondent, unhappy, negative path. Why would we choose the latter? (And she has learned that it really does all come down to choice.) It takes a conscious act of will to pull oneself out of the depth of despair. Sharing with someone who is willing to listen can be the first step in making progress. "The best way out is through it," says Sam. "That means going through the muck, talking and analyzing what got you there in the first place, so you can begin to heal and, hopefully, avoid the pitfalls the next time. Then, accepting what didn't work and beginning again in a better state of mind. The ultimate source of happiness has got to come from within. Our mental attitude controls ninety-nine percent of it. That mental attitude is nourished by people, things, and activities. Knowing yourself and knowing what makes you happy, what motivates you, what fulfills you is the key." In Sam's life creativity is very important as it gives her self-satisfaction, a feel good response to something unsettling. When all else fails, however, cleaning and rearranging furniture usually works wonders and tires her out so her mind can rest along with her body. "I stay busy with family, daily trips to the gym, reading, crafts and sewing, and when the day ends I treat myself to an evening of television."

"I have found the best way to accept failure and disappointment is to sulk a little and then stop thinking about myself and reach out to help someone else. Easier said than done! Especially those of us who hate to make mistakes. Life is one adjustment after another to changes, aging, grief, trauma, or anything difficult to deal with. How we handle those adjustments has a lot to say about the kind of person we are," concludes Sam.

Now it's back to me, Nadine. I have a theory that the vast majority of human beings mature automatically both physically and mentally unless there is a major obstacle making that impossible (mental or physical diseases). Bodies grow on their own, and almost all people learn to read, write, do arithmetic and attain all the skills necessary to function in society. Emotional maturation is a very different thing. I don't begin to know the reasons, but it appears to me that people can, and many do, stop their emotional growth at various stages of development. I know that addiction treatment includes the information that when people start using, whether it's alcohol or drugs, they stop their emotional growth. I have also read that when young people (don't know how young) start having sex or when a girl has a baby they stop growing emotionally. It seems to me that adolescence is the most common time for emotional stoppage, which would correspond with the having sex or having a baby theory. The evidence to which I point in support of my theory is (1) my association with many, many people in my 79 years, (2) what passes for humor by adults on television, AND (3) the behavior of our leaders in this country. They are supposed to be the best and the brightest, and they might be mentally, but there's that emotional maturity (or lack thereof) again.

Anyway, when I was in my early 40s I came to the conclusion that I was functioning on the emotions of a teenager. One of my friends told me that her therapist had made the statement that most people don't update the information upon which they function. That was definitely me. How could 17-year-old ideas still be appropriate for a 40-something mother of six? So I began the practice of putting my thoughts to the "are they current (?)," "still relevant (?)" tests. I'm sure this was the start of what would eventually be a divorce. More than once over the years I have wondered if getting a divorce was the right thing to do, or was it perhaps not working harder to find a replacement, as I have now been alone for a large portion of my life. But the truth is, it has been important for me to remain single so that I could continue to work toward that emotional maturity of which I speak. My immediate response to having a partner was to lose sight of myself and become an appendage of his. It took some years and a couple more relationships to figure that one out.

Although it turned out that the divorce was the very best thing for me, it wasn't an easy process. I cried every day for six months. Having a job to be responsible to was a lifesaver. It gave me a focus outside myself. It also gave me a mirror to my mood swings. One day someone would not say "Good morning" to me and I would be mad about that. The next day someone would say "Good morning" to me and I would wonder why. The final straw was one afternoon that I remember as though it was yesterday. I was curled up in a fetal position, in my pajamas, lying on top of the furnace vent, rocking back and forth, crying and wondering "what's it all about," when I was hit with the thought: I can either stay like this and end up in the looney bin or get up and get out and get on with life. Ever so gradually things began to get better.

I think most people who have known me over the years would say that I'm a happy person. I think I'm a happy person. But that happiness has needed some propping up from time to time. I definitely believe that aging has its challenges for maintaining good mental and emotional health. When you feel that you have done all you wanted to do, no longer have anything you can or want to reach for, no longer have a significant place in society or just your own family, and in many respects are just marking time, depression seems to be around the next corner. My experience working in mental health taught me that depression often comes disguised as dementia. So I stay alert to both possibilities. Antidepressants work wonders and don't have to be forever. If needed, I'll take them.

So I make quilts, do counted cross-stitch, knit and crochet and enjoy it all very much. I read, mostly nonfiction, and have been studying "A Course in Miracles" for several years. I make my own greeting cards, with the assistance of a computer program from Hallmark, and I make a family calendar every year which becomes my Christmas gift to 15 people. I belong to two organizations for which I maintain the books and through which I have made some new friends. I meet with a group of high school friends for lunch once monthly as I do with the threesome writing this book. My daughter owns a small restaurant in a small town and I polish and wrap the silverware for her which takes a couple hours 5 days a week. Being in the restaurant so frequently has given me the opportunity to become acquainted with several people my age which has also been enjoyable for me.

From a purely mental standpoint I have always been a clear and logical thinker, and I remain so today. Occasionally, I notice that I have to search for a word, most often it's a name, or I have what I call a "skipped synapse." That simply means that I have thought something bothersome as a result of not connecting two things/thoughts together properly, i.e., worrying about how to get the water line hooked to the new refrigerator, when the new refrigerator does not have an ice maker, so no water line is needed. Or, thinking I will have to leave the cabin a day early because there are no eggs for breakfast the next morning rather than thinking I can run to the store for eggs or I can have something other than eggs for breakfast. At least, so far, these incidents become cause for laughter. Let's hope it continues thus.

At the present time, I'm in the process of planning my 80th birthday party which will actually be a family reunion for me and my sisters' children, grandchildren and greats; the first in 15 years. I am having such fun preparing things and planning all the details, that it has become clear to me the need for having something to think about, something to do, something to look forward to. And therein lies the formula for happiness that I only heard recently while watching TV; (1) having something to do, (2) having something to love, and (3) having something to look forward to. So, the challenge will be keeping this going after the party.

Oh, and there's one more thing. I would like to say "Amen" to Mary Jo and Sam's contributions to this chapter.

They both demonstrate through their life experiences the very things that I, as a therapist, tried to get people to understand and incorporate into their lives.

Chapter Three
Love, Marriage and Family

"Being a family means you are part of something very wonderful. It means you will love and be loved the rest of your life."

Lisa Weed

In writing a chapter on Love, Marriage, and Family we have all had a similar, yet different, experience: all married but two divorced. Similar in as far as we all started out with the same goals, hopes, and determination. You fall in love, you get married, you start a family. Our generation generally had the wife at home while the husband worked. We looked after the children, cooked all the meals, did all the laundry, shopping, and carpooling. A lot of the housework was shared by having the children do their chores for a small allowance once a week. We expected life to continue down that path with not too many hurdles. Human nature as it is, however, made for consequences that we didn't see coming, and each of us had to learn how to navigate through many years of trial and error, happiness and sorrow, success and failure, and all of us with unplanned heartache. There was no lesson plan to show us how to cope. Forty years ago none of us would have guessed how each of us were to fare in the years ahead, so when we were united again it was with great shock and amazement to find out how things had transpired. As the only "still married" member of this group I, Sam, have the privilege of presenting this chapter.

Nadine starts us off. She says, historically speaking, combining love, marriage and family are rather recent concepts. Certainly within the last 150 years. But, by the 1950s the concept was predominant throughout the American culture. Following are lyrics to the song "Love and Marriage," introduced by Frank Sinatra in 1955:

Love and marriage, love and marriage
Go together like a horse and carriage
This I tell you, brother
You can't have one without the other.

"In my case," she says, "I claim to have been in love twice so far in this lifetime. The first was with my high school sweetheart, the man I married, with whom I have six children, and from whom I was divorced after 30 years of marriage. Love does not solve all problems. Love is not 'all you need' nor is it what 'makes the world go 'round.'"

Nadine believes that love is glamorized and misrepresented in our society. For the most part, what is referred to as love is lust; at least in the case of love that involves sexual expression. Love for your parents and children are probably closer to real love. She emphasizes her belief that love for children is as close as we can come to "unconditional" love, if that is even possible. She continues with her belief that the love of which Jesus spoke; i.e. "Love your enemies" and "As the Father has loved me, I love you" could not possibly be the love of Valentine's Day and the American culture. Perhaps the word "love" has evolved into something other than it meant in Jesus' time. In any case, she proposes that we use the word respect in its place. "I can, and do, respect everyone in my world. At least that is my intent," she says.

Nadine continues with: "We married way too young. I was 17 and he was 20. I was pregnant. For the duration of the marriage that was his reason for getting married. Not that he loved me. Not that he wanted to marry me. Only that I was pregnant and that it was the 'right thing to do.' When we finally divorced he said, 'Well, I never loved you anyway.' Ouch!! It's no wonder that the marriage could never become a union of two loving souls. One was not there. I think I would say to this day that I love him, but I grew to not like him.

"The children that resulted from that union are priceless. I love each and every one of them, and I believe, more importantly, that I like each of them. I have always maintained that I would have had six more had their father been as invested as I was." They were her biggest concern when divorce was imminent. Perhaps more accurately, she was concerned for the future of "the family." She and her husband did agree before the final separation that they would do their best to have their behaviors affect the children as little as possible. They agreed that the two of them would come together for family occasions, i.e., Christmas, Thanksgiving, birthdays, weddings, etc., so that the children could see that their parents could be civil with each other and that there was family continuity. She feels that, for the most part, that worked well.

Nadine says, "I originally stated that I don't know what these adult children would say now about the effects of the divorce on their lives. However, I have since asked and they all feel that they were definitely affected, not to the point of trauma, but affected, even though the youngest was 18 years old. And for sure, I can say that the effects were overwhelmingly positive for me! As painful as it was at the time, I knew it would ultimately be a good thing. I guess this is where people have the debate of whether it is better to sacrifice self for the good of the whole, or not. And, if after you have made that sacrifice, was it actually better for the whole?"

By the way, her second love was the reuniting of old friends after her divorce. He was still married so it did not lead to another marriage and the actual togetherness only lasted six months. "I maintain that I learned so much from that relationship that it was worth the heartbreak I experienced as a result," says Nadine.

Following is something Nadine wrote in 1977 on the topic of love. The family had moved from her home of 35 years to California. She was hoping the geographical change would affect a change in the marriage. It did not. She was adjusting to a new environment, observing a new group of friends and pondering just what is love, settling for what people call love.

IT ALL DEPENDS ON
YOUR DEFINITION OF LOVE—I GUESS

<u>*Consider the Sweetheart*</u>
I love her, therefore
I hold her accountable for my feelings;
I expect her to fulfill my hopes and dreams;
I will make her happy;
I need her.

<u>*Consider the Wife*</u>
I love him, therefore
I decide what's best for him;
I defend his mistakes;
I allow myself to be his excuse;
I like his likes, think his thoughts, dream his dreams.

<u>*Consider the Parent*</u>
I love them, therefore
I protect them from failure;
I ignore their shortcomings;
I assume their responsibilities;
I expect them to be something.

<u>*Consider the Masters*</u>
I love you, therefore
I accept you just the way you are;
I will show you the way to your highest potential,
The choice to follow is yours;
I will laugh with you, cry with you, share myself with you;
I will die with you that we might live.

Mary Jo says that after years of pondering the problems within her marriage, to no avail, it was difficult, at this time, to go back to that time and reflect on it all over again. But she's willing to share what she has determined to be the cause and effect of those times.

In her marriage, she says, as in all marriages, we bring the wounds of growing up with us. Her husband was the oldest child followed by four siblings. His role was to be the protector, as his father was in the Navy and away during those early years. His mother favored his brother and was kept busy with the three sisters. He needed to be number one and the favorite and couldn't get enough attention and support. Mary Jo, on the other hand, said she was in the mindset that one had to earn love and acceptance through obedience and service.

She continues, saying that the first few years were perfect in their marriage. Their needs were fulfilled in one another. It was strained a bit when the first child was born. Her motherly instinct was strong, and her son became her primary focus. Her husband felt betrayed and constantly competed for attention. As other children arrived, he felt alienated from the family as his need was no longer being fulfilled. "I remember being confused by his reactions and thought to myself that my need was to have a partner, not another child. We continued to be respectful and kind to one another, although our basic needs were no longer being met."

The distance between them grew without much awareness of it happening. He stayed busy with his work and she with the children. Their fun and support came from friends. They had a small group of close friends and did a lot of casual entertaining. Neither of them could communicate the frustrations they felt and, after several futile attempts, drifted into indifference. They gave up trying to make things work and sought their needs in social gatherings. Looking back, she says, it is no wonder that he found another to love him. This woman didn't like children, had few friends, disliked his mother and siblings, and made him the total focus of their relationship. Her ex-husband and his new wife's world narrowed down to just the two of them. He sold his business and ended up with less stressful work. "I have to believe that he was finally happy," stated Mary Jo.

As for Mary Jo, she says it took several years to heal from the rejection, but through children and friends she found a new life, one that included nursing, a social life with single friends, and eventually retirement and taking care of grandchildren. So her most basic needs were finally met, too. "I had lost respect for him when he divorced the children as well as me. It made it easier to go on with my life because without respect it is very difficult to keep love in a relationship. It is only when you work together as equals and accept the differences in your personalities that marriage can grow and thrive. If one has to take a lesser role in the union, it can lead to indifference and eventually the death of love."

Mary Jo acknowledges that family is so important. Growing up, your parents and siblings play a major role in your development. "I have touched on my parents in other chapters so will not dwell on it. As for my siblings, my older brother was not thrilled to have two younger sisters. He kept apart from us for a good part of the time. But scouting mountaintops with him as a guide is one good memory. We regarded him as a "star." He was always kind but a little distant. We became closer as adults. My sister and I shared a bedroom. We were constant companions and grew up being very close. Only with marriages and families did we go our separate ways. My younger brother was 14 years younger than me. I was old enough to think I was his second mother. I took him everywhere that I could, told him bedtime stories, and just adored him. I left home for college when he was four years old. I think my sister rejoiced when I left so she could enjoy a closeness with him, also. It wasn't until we lost our parents, our brother, and our sister that we reunited. Although we live a long way apart, we enjoy talking on the phone and sharing memories from our past. Now he is a comfort and a friend. What could be better?"

As for her children, she mentioned that their father abandoned them as well as her. Mary Jo said that the only good thing from that experience was that the children and she bonded together in support and love. They have their ups and downs but are always there for one another. "My younger son, because of his past, is one terrific dad. All four children have turned out to be great adults. I am proud of them all and consider them my friends. They are kind, thoughtful, loyal, and respectful (qualities I hold dear)."

"What I have learned through my marriage and divorce is that I, too, had my own shortcomings. I once, for a short time, dated a man that was much like my ex-husband. He was polite, intelligent, kind, and good looking. My reaction to him showed me my own failures of character. I regarded him as my superior so was afraid to speak my mind. I must be good and earn his love. Bad habit! The relationship didn't last long, but I learned a lot about myself. It became clear to me that it was as a single woman that I could be me and accept me as I am. It lead to self-worth and happiness. Over the years, I have grown stronger and more confident in who I am. Is it a matter of aging? If so, embrace it. For with it comes a certain peace," concludes Mary Jo.

As the last of our threesome on this topic I, Sam, have the audacity to have remained married for going on 57 years!!! I am the first to tell you that it is a combination of love, determination, stubbornness, finances, five children, tolerance, history, fear, and so many more things that go into a marital relationship that may or may not keep it going.

In the era of us 70- to 80-year-olds, love and marriage began at a much earlier age than it does today. The advantage of that, at least for me was that I was too young and naïve to know what I'd gotten into. But it did give me more energy for kids and, later on, for grandkids. And now, in retrospect, I can enjoy great grandkids as well as some quality "senior" time if I can maintain a somewhat healthy body and lifestyle.

Of course the downside to a young marriage (and the three of us have all experienced some degree of it) is that we started out with meager beginnings and added children right away which left a sense of always wanting and needing "more." It takes time to establish a career, buy a house, the necessities of life, and whoever heard of "date night" or "saving for retirement" back then!

Our social life consisted of getting together with friends to play cards or board games with treats for the evening of popcorn and Kool-Aid. Most activities included the children because we couldn't afford a babysitter. We really thought we were doing well when we advanced to soda pop and eventually beer! When I asked my Mom what it was like during the Great Depression, she said everyone was in the same boat so they didn't think much of it. I guess that's where our mentality was, also. We were so busy with everyday family life we didn't spend much time on the real meaning of what it takes to sustain a GOOD marriage.

The blessings of our five children is such a gift from God. They were good students, good athletes, kept out of trouble and drugs, and made us proud to be their parents. To see how they have grown into well-adjusted, responsible, loving parents to our 16 grandchildren leaves me in complete awe. And all five of them have maintained first and lasting marriages and done well in each of their professions. How does that happen in this day and age? We are truly blessed. They are, most likely, the reason we've stayed married all these years!

I have realized that there should be five powerful, necessary qualities practiced in a marriage, which can also pertain to family, friends, and careers. Those universal attributes are honesty, humor, respect, communication, and love. It seems that missing any one of those can cause such dysfunction in a relationship if it is not addressed, and my marriage has had to deal with more than one.

The hurt and unfairness in a relationship happens when one or both parties forgets those things and then, when faced with them, refuses to sit down and discuss how things can be made right. The results can be devastating with built-up animosity. It begins to grow like a cancer if put off too long. When you finally say "that's enough" three things can happen: you can fix it, you can get a divorce, or you can continue down the road you're on and hope that changes can be made.

As humans we are adaptable and learn to adjust to the lives we've become accustomed to. Unfortunately, that can be an awful way to live. So we seek other ways and other people to fill the gap. Our children become more important to us than our spouse. Regret rears its ugly head. By the time we figure it all out we've spent years of trying to keep it together and, once again, we are at the place of "just surviving." Surely we should be able to do more than that!

I was fortunate enough to be the beneficiary of four older siblings; two who were 14 years older; 2 who were 10 years older; all twins. My only sister was like a second mother. She spent time teaching me nursery rhymes and reading me books when I was little. When I got married we became best friends. The 14-year age difference shortened considerably. I had the advantage of learning from her mistakes and willingly took her advice. It saved me more times than I could count as I had enough to handle making my own mistakes. At this stage of my life I find myself thinking of her, my brothers, and my folks very often and wishing we could have had more time.

It's interesting to me to see the similarities in my siblings and me and then in my children and me. There are things that I believe we have no control over no matter how much we dislike them in ourselves or try to change them. I can't seem to make the corrections even though I'd like to. And when I see those faults in my children, I wish I could help them. I guess it's necessary for all of us to experience the "cause-and-effect syndrome" in each of our lives to learn our lessons and perhaps keep us humble. But sometimes it hurts! We become a mature adult when we no longer blame our parents for the faults in ourselves. Reflecting on only the good things is a better way to deal with the negative. It certainly helps to realize none of us are perfect, and we must accept everyone as they are. Of course, some are more acceptable than others!

So, how do we live with the same person for most of our life? I realize my two friends have stated how happy they are to be single and not have to deal with those spousal interactions. But one of the good things (but not always easy) is how we hold each other accountable in our thinking, opinions, and actions. Who can do that without all the bumps and hurts? Obviously, we have to learn how to make things work in order to (here's that word again!) survive. Or, at least, make them work for whatever is unique to us. It's hard, it's unpleasant at times, and it takes more than some of us can give. I can only hope that our trials and tribulations will pan out at the end. A lifetime of sticking it out does have some positive and pleasant rewards. After giving up on my husband not being willing to fly to Europe, he came home one day and surprised me by saying he was taking me on a riverboat trip down the Rhine River from the Netherlands to Germany to France to Switzerland!! WOW!! So, there is an unexpected and pleasant reward worth waiting for. I began packing (in my head) immediately!

Not knowing what each day will bring is a constant adventure, and, I must say that if I knew then what I know now, I probably still would have done it all the same anyway. Isn't that a kick in the head?

Chapter Four
Friends, Pets and Relationships

Truly great friends are hard to find, difficult to leave, and impossible to forget. A true friend is someone who thinks that you are a good egg even though he knows that you are slightly cracked.

Bernard Meltzer

I, Mary Jo, admit that this is my favorite chapter, so I'm delighted to be the facilitator of it. However, Sam leads off the discussion as she is our action person. She shows an eagerness and desire to get going. So here she goes.

What defines a "friend"? She has had many throughout her life that she considered a friend. The dictionary says "a friend is a person one knows, likes, and trusts; a favored companion; comrade." Since she considers herself to be a pretty trusting person she has allowed a lot of people into her life and called them "friend." What concerns her is that they have all come and gone over the years. No one person has become a "constant." "But now, two of them have returned after forty years. FORTY YEARS!" Sam exclaims. "And they seem to accept and like me, even with all my flaws! I think we become way more tolerant and less critical of others as we grow older, realizing that we're not too perfect ourselves."

That being said, Sam admits that she found the opposite sex to be more to her liking as friends in her earlier years. "My husband was my best friend before we married which I guess was a good way to begin our marriage. I've always had a large interest in the sports world and have been able to communicate with men in that regard. However, my confidants over the years have been mostly women, with the exception of a couple of men who seem to be more in touch with their feminine side," Sam stated.

As stated in a previous chapter, Sam thinks the most important things in any relationship should be HUMOR, TRUST, HONESTY, RESPECT, and LOVE. It is truly devastating when any or all of those virtues are lost or abused in a friendship. A person who can respond, forgive, and bounce back with someone who has knowingly, or even unintentionally, abused one of those qualities is someone worthy of keeping and calling a "friend."

In chatting with her morning workout friends at coffee, Sam discovered that only one in the seven of them had kept up with not only one but several lifetime friends on a regular basis. Sam found that very unique and thought this person was truly blessed to have that kind of experience in her life. That takes an effort on one's part to sustain, and most of us don't put that kind of time into it. However, Sam and her husband are part of a unique group of their high school classmates from the late 1950s and early 1960s who are still meeting at quarterly luncheons and have an email correspondence to keep them all apprised of what's going on, mostly obituaries at this stage! The only problem is that their friends are 900 miles "back home" so they only get there once a year. But what fun when they do. The stories get told over and over again and with more embellishment each time they're told! Age and forgetfulness are a cause for a lot of laughs.

"Being friends with my children has been a 'plus' I didn't know I would have when I began having children," states Sam. "However, I've learned that as unique as each of them is, I've had to respond differently to each of them because of their different personalities. One is more sensitive, one is more dominant, one is more critical, one is more opinionated, and one is more insecure. They all have a lot of really wonderful traits, but when dealing with the aforementioned moods, and each can resemble any of those at any time, I just need to be aware and respond to them in a way that preserves our relationship. They are precious to me and I love them all the same. I LIKE some of them better than others, and that is subject to change regularly! They know this and laugh at me."

Sam has had different friends at different times in her life, and for different circumstances, and connections made that only she and that person had in common. Whenever they get together their bond is based on the history they've shared. Each friend has a different story about their relationship. There is no "one" person who has shared "everything" with her nor she with them. "And I most likely will never have a friend who knows all my dark secrets," states Sam. "However, if they were all in one place at one time and decided to share what they know of me, the complete tale could possibly be told. And, oh, what a story that would be!"

"Who in their life hasn't done something they are ashamed of and would hesitate to share with anyone?" continues Sam. "I would sometimes like to bare my soul regarding those things but would hate to possibly change that person's opinion of me. However, 'it's not their job to like me, it's mine.' And I've needed to forgive myself many times and move on. I've learned that a real friend will love you in spite of yourself."

This brings Sam to the most loving, accepting, and eager constants in her life; Yogi and Bear: a 15-year-old toy poodle and a 5-year-old Yorkie. "Two yahoos who took years to realize that there wasn't a secret exit door in the bathroom for me to escape from, but took only seconds to learn the words treat, walk, car, and bye-bye," says Sam. If only we humans could learn that unconditional love that dogs have. Although Sam believes she has it with them most of the time. "Did you know that when you look at them or touch them with that wonderful feeling of how much you love them, you actually have a chemical release of, I guess the word would be, endorphins?" according to Sam. Everyone in Sam's family has at least one dog. Each have become another one of her "friends." But not until the children were grown and left Sam and her husband did she appreciate the comfort that their two pups have brought them.

"Speaking of children and their leaving home, in my family the cliché 'Empty Nest Syndrome' became a very real thing and almost caused our (my husband and myself) lifelong friendship to dissolve. When there is less of everything (laundry, cleaning, cooking, activities, conversation, etc.), there needs to be more of something else to replace it. Until we realized what the problem was, it took us a while to fix it. But eventually we settled into a new routine that worked."

Sam admires the distinctive qualities in her different friends and tends to gravitate to those with specific talents. "They are always amazing to me. I appreciate that each one of them has their own gifts to share with the rest of us. And I am thankful that they're all in my life," concludes Sam.

I, Mary Jo, find it very hard to listen without interrupting because Sam's comments stimulate my own journeys and thoughts regarding my friends. However, I listened quietly. Then Nadine decided to share her thoughts. She adds a lot to our discussions. As a psychologist she tends to make us dig a little deeper into ourselves.

The importance of friends in her life cannot be overstated. She has been working on "My Story" for several years now to be left for/given to her children. The essence of this story is the people in her life including her friends over the years, from grammar school to the present time. (Several of her friendships started in the 2nd grade and lasted until their deaths.) The friends invited to her 80th birthday celebration date back to high school.

"Having been the youngest of 3 girls by 6 and 7 years, I was very much the 'afterthought' with no partner in the family. For as long as I can remember I looked outside the home for companionship. I found support, encouragement, praise, fun and laughter in all kinds of relationships from friends my own age to adults in various roles. As an adult myself I added working relationships which, although most were never in the 'friends' category, were always essential to my attitude about and enjoyment of my various work environments. Ultimately even those students/clients/ patients for whom I provided services became valued relationships," Nadine shared.

Even during the extremely tough times in life, a financial disaster and a divorce, there was at least one friend ready and willing to stand with Nadine. One of the most difficult times was when the two people she counted on the most in times of joy or sorrow, both long distance but usually available by phone, died within a month of each other. (One was her next older sister with whom she had become very close in the previous two years, and the other was a friend of 40+ years who would be the closest to what Nadine would ever call a best friend.) "Now what do I do?" Nadine wondered. "Who do I lean on when the two people I have leaned on are gone? They were never replaced, but life went on. I kept telling myself there's a message in here somewhere. Perhaps it's time for me to depend on myself, to lean on me."

During all her years of friendships and relationships on different levels there was never one with whom she could talk about everything. With this one she avoided politics, with that one she avoided religion, and with another one she avoided anything of an intimate nature. With all of them she avoided anything about which she felt shame. "There are secrets I have held to this day that I have never told another soul," states Nadine.

"At least not a human soul. But let me tell you about my dogs. They are Bichons, born 3 days apart (same kennel, different litters). Koko is a girl and Kasper is a boy. They were five years old this February. If all goes well their ashes will be added with mine at the end. (I actually have the ashes of a former pair of Bichons, Kream and Sugar, to be added also.) These dogs have been my companions through singlehood, through learning to live alone in my fifties after a failed attempt at another relationship, through returning to an education some four decades late, through job changes and household moves, and finally into my present-day retirement. I love these dogs, and I tell them so on a regular basis. I can't imagine a better therapy for all people but certainly for elderly people. They give me the responsibility of caring for another, they show me their love and loyalty at all times, and they listen attentively to all I have to say and never betray the trust I have placed in them, and THEY – MAKE – ME – LAUGH, a lot!"

Having said all that Nadine says she does believe that if the circumstances were right she would today share everything with this threesome. "There is something about being on the final chapter of my life that allows me, even encourages me to get it all out. To let people know exactly who I am and to accept without reservation who they are. I can't put a value on that."

Now it is my turn. (We're back to Mary Jo.) Where to begin regarding relationships? Growing up, I was the second of four children and first daughter. I am convinced that your place in the family has significant value in who you become. I felt it was my duty to protect my sister although she was only 14 months younger. My motherly instinct grew stronger and dominated my life and all relationships.

It was a secure home, a happy home, with very little strife as long as you were obedient children. And all four of us were just that. I do remember as a child thinking, "It's okay to have opinions other than those of your parents. Just don't voice them." It sort of summed up my stance in all relationships. "Peace at any price," but it turned out to be too high of a price.

I found my comfort in one or two close friends as I entered my school years. Certainly my sister was my constant companion and closest friend. In high school, it was down to one close friend and a small group of casual friends. Even when the family moved to a very small town during my sophomore and junior years, I had one dear friend and many casual friends. That one friend has lasted a lifetime. The nice thing about small towns is that new faces are welcomed with open arms. It was a wonderful experience. In those days there were was no alcohol, smoking, or drugs, not even a thought, and only innocent fun. A youth group in the church, school activities, ice skating, or picnics depending on the season. Yes, those who had cars filled them with us who did not, and burned the point. It didn't take long to cruise three or four blocks.

College was my first taste of freedom, although it was a Catholic school with strict hours. My history carried true to form with one close friend, but I had several good friends (both female and male). It was a fun year, and then off to nursing school for the next 2 years. The hospital became my home away from home, and I loved every department and the people I worked with (except for a few nasty RNs).

My most important relationship in my life was with my husband. We were both just finishing college about the same time and facing an uncertain future. It was comforting to have someone with whom to plan a future. I don't think either of us felt that "in-love" experience. It simply was the time to get married and enter a life expected of us. As I elaborated on this in Chapter 3, I won't go any further but to say that after 30 years he lost his wife and made amends to his family, his children and me. Hence, forgiveness!

I never remarried. Since I really didn't know what went wrong in our marriage, I was afraid to give myself fully to another. Only hindsight and forgiveness are needed for a healthy relationship.

Friendships come and go according to the state of life we are experiencing. We (my husband and I) had a group of friends from our church and the parochial school our children attended. At the time of our marital problems, the majority of those friends avoided us both as they stated they didn't want to pick sides. One friend from another town flew in to go with me to the lawyer. She just wanted to be there as support. Another friend invited me to several social gatherings at her home. She would come over to visit just to be there for me.

Another friend asked me to join a group dealing with relationships, a group that developed close ties and lasted for years. One of the women in that group was a nun who had some difficulties in her life so she came to live with me, a situation that was on and off for about 10 years. She became a dear friend and was so loved by my family that she was considered part of the family. She and several other women from the group have since passed, but one Native American woman and I remain close to this day.

I renewed my friendship with a woman who was in nursing school with me. She was there for me while I was in the medical rehab facility and afterwards to drive to the various doctor visits. She was my angel of mercy when I most needed one. She remains a close friend and has taught me what it takes to be a true friend.

My church friends have been there for me also and we continued to go to Mass together, followed by breakfast out. On hold for now due to the pandemic.

I have remained friends with some of the people with whom I worked. We don't schedule a routine time but, when we do get together we do have a good laugh remembering some of the episodes in our work.

The most valuable relationships in my life now are with my children. I loved being a mother. They fulfilled me totally. The teen years weren't my favorite, but thankfully we all survived them intact. One of the greatest things for a mother is when your children become adults and you are so proud of the characters of each one.

As my children grew up and entered adult lives, they gave me grandchildren. But they too grew up, and suddenly I was very much alone for the very first time. So I decided to get a puppy. Dudley is a Dachshund/ Miniature Schnauzer mix. I have always had dogs and cats when raising a family. As much as I loved them, they were pets! Dudley at this stage of my life became almost like my child. I apologize when leaving him alone. I talk everything over with him. Finally, there was that unconditional love we all seek. He accepts me with all my warts and moods and never leaves my side. He is so smart. I'm sure my other dogs were, too, but we never gave them enough attention to realize how much they understood. He is my companion and only asks for loving (or belly rubs), a walk, a ride in the car now and then, and treats. He is a nut and makes me laugh often during the day with his antics. He fills that empty spot in my life. What a joy!!

It made me realize how valuable my close friends are. I have never needed many, just a few good friends whom you can share the good and the bad times and trust them with your thoughts. I have been graced with just that throughout my life. It was close friends that were the source of my happiness while married. It was close friends that saw me through the adjustments to single life. And it is close friends that see me through the later years of life. We are all blessed when we have one or two such friends. The three of us are discovering these truths now.

The bottom line is that I have had two separate lives in one. One of marriage and motherhood, which was a life full of family and friends. One full of trips, summers at the cabin and parties with friends. The second half was as a single woman. I went back to nursing, loving every minute of it. Then I retired to take care of my grandchildren. Love personified. The rewards are that we are all so close. Cousins are more like siblings. They filled my life with purpose and laughter and fun and love.

I am grateful for a life full of family and friends. I am grateful to be physically and financially independent. I am grateful for my whole life.

Chapter Five
Sex, Money and Power

We don't get smarter about sex, money and power as we get older, we just don't have enough stamina to care.

Authors' Quote

Observations of human history make it clear that sex, money and power are the driving forces for the human species. Therefore, we thought it appropriate to speak about them in reference to being old. There is no sex, little money and, therefore, no power…. On to the next topic. Ha-ha. Not so. This might be my least favorite chapter, but I guess I drew the short straw for presenting it. Nadine.

Let's start this chapter with Sam's comments. She's not sure what to write about on any of these topics since she says she's never had much of any one of them. She's going to speak of each of them separately even though they all work hand in hand for many people. She starts her comments with: "Sex, money and power are and always have been a global pandemic. They cause all the problems on earth. But, for the purposes of this book I am writing how they affect me personally, each one being a predominant issue at any one time throughout my life."

She continues with her belief that, "We start out with sex being utmost in our minds when our bodies begin to change. Puberty, experimentation, dating, young adulthood, and early years of marriage seem to put sex at the top of most people's 'to do' list. People have always been curious about something new and the unknown and young pubescents are no different. Our generation wasn't instructed on the intricacies of what to do with hormonal feelings so we were left with trial and error." She wishes she would have had better teaching of how to fulfill her partner's pleasure, and explain to her partner what her needs were. She feels it would have saved a lot of frustration and hurt. Although she always enjoyed sex, it took a lot of years to figure out how much more enjoyable it could be when done "right." She supposes she is just as much at fault as her parents were in not instructing her children in those intricacies of sex, and "I hope they have all found out by now what they needed to know to make it great. They probably have and it's only me who was the uneducated one!" My mother-in-law once told me that sex pretty much stops at age fifty and I laughed prematurely at THAT comment!

When speaking of money, Sam starts with, "Unfortunately it's a necessity of life. Too little of it or too much of it can cause just as many problems." She says that as a young married couple she and her husband seldom had enough to make ends meet while raising a large family. She clipped coupons, sewed much of their wardrobe, hunted and fished for their food, and bargain-shopped for everything she could. Those days were a frustration for her, but the kids learned to work hard for what they wanted and appreciated everything they got. Nothing was handed to them so "I guess being poor was a good thing." The kids couldn't afford to get into drugs, there was no car for them to drive, and they were kept busy with sports and other activities, so they had no time to get into trouble. "As parents we wished we could have done better. I suppose every generation wished that and, as far as I can tell, each succeeding generation has done better for their children. As poor as I was raised, my kids, as little as they had, had much more. And my grandchildren seem to lack for nothing!"

Sam was finally able to work full time when she no longer had to be at home to take care of small children. So they managed to get them raised, into college, and out of the house. However, that all happened AFTER they had to sell the house, their car was repossessed, and her husband lost his job. "If that doesn't put a stress on your life and your marriage, I don't know what else does! We survived it, put it behind us, and moved on. We moved on to kids' marriages, grandchildren, and now retirement and great grandchildren. Moneywise we're comfortable but physically we're limited with what we can do with it!!" laughs Sam.

Sam believes that power struggles happen in every relationship when one person (or country for that matter) wants to have their own way, or thinks their way is better. "I know our marriage wouldn't have had as many 'power' problems if communication was better. I believe most problems can be solved if the parties are willing to communicate. Most of us don't consciously want to take over and dominate our spouse because we know it can lead to real unhappiness when things are one sided. When they say marriage is a 50-50 deal it should really be said it's a 100 percent thing; sometimes 60-40, sometimes 70-30, sometimes 80-20, and sometimes 90-10. But ALWAYS, both people putting in 100% of themselves." She continues by saying she's not sure people were intended to live the majority of their lives with one other person. It's hard and sometimes for the sanctity of both parties you have to get out of the relationship to survive losing yourself altogether. She feels that if she wasn't a strong person she would have escaped long ago. "The children would have survived because, unless you've done a really crappy job of parenting, they're going to understand. And most kids are so wrapped up in their own lives that they're not going to be too concerned about yours. In my own case, leaving would have put a much graver financial burden on us than the one we were already in."

Sam's final comments on this topic follow. "I found that the most beneficial of the three things of sex, money, and power for me turned out to be power, in so much as power in my case is what I consider as strength. It was my own power/strength to be able to 'hang in there' for 56+ years of marriage. The power/strength I had to keep hoping. Hoping things could improve. Hoping things would change. Because I loved my husband I tried to accommodate his wishes and decisions and in so doing gave him power that he didn't know how to handle, or was even aware of, and everything has been off center ever since. Being a 'glass half full' instead of a 'glass half empty' kind of person has kept me hoping that change would come and things would get better. Sometimes they did, sometimes they didn't. I learned that nothing stays the same. Just wait 24 hours and I will see something different. In the meantime, I learned to compensate with things that fulfilled me. And there were many, many things that did that. So, life goes on and some of those things fill the void of those parts that need, or needed, filling. Maybe that's the best anyone can hope for. It doesn't make for happiness, but it does bring acceptance."

And now it's Mary Jo's turn. "We all agreed that sex should be discussed as we were all married and it is a vital component of marriage." She proceeds by addressing the different attitudes in our astrological signs. She saw the truth in each sign indicating that her sign reflects her attitude towards sex. "While I enjoyed the pleasures of sexual contact, it was more than that to me. It represented the emotional union as well as the physical. It was good to be held tight, to enjoy the intimacy of the moment." When she discussed this with others she became aware that to some, it is simply pleasure and means nothing more than sexual gratification. Again, for Mary Jo, it depends on one's astrological sign. For example, with the Scorpio, sex is just sex and to be enjoyed. "But I am a

Cancer, and sex means much more. Emotions are an intricate part of it. It is an expression of love, a comfort, a binding of souls and bodies. Fortunately, for me, my husband was a Cancer also. However, after being married for decades, sex became just sex—a physical release—had little to do with that emotional contact. So, enough about sex."

The subject of money is a bit more complex for Mary Jo. She grew up in a family where money was not abundant. They actually lived monthly paycheck to paycheck. Yet, as a child, she never realized how her parents struggled. She always felt she was well fed, well dressed, and had all her basic needs met. It wasn't until she was married and with children that she realized how well her mother had managed their home and her budget. Mary Jo had new insight with an attitude of gratitude for her mother and respect for how she managed on a limited income.

As a young single woman just out of college, Mary Jo lived from paycheck to paycheck, surviving only because "four of us shared the costs of a rental home, and groceries. These were fun years, and I never considered myself to be deprived in any way," she says. After marriage, her husband worked for his father in a family business. He started at the bottom to learn every aspect of the business. His paycheck reflected the position he held. Even though she became pregnant right away, she continued to work at the hospital (remember she's a Registered Nurse) until their first child was born. "My paycheck went to pay off my college loan so we struggled a bit to adjust to his income. Once our son was born, money was even tighter. We both looked back on those years as the best years of our marriage. I was a 'stay-at-home mom.' We talked and worked together. It wasn't until his father passed away and the business became his to run that stress entered our lives." By then they had four children, so she was busy being a mother and doing some volunteer work. With the stress of running a business and so little attention at home, her husband was just trying to exist and maintain somewhat of a normal life. He became emotionally distant and when she tried to communicate with him, it was in vain. So the increase of money did not bring happiness. Mary Jo states that, "It was a comfort to know that we could pay all the bills, put money in savings and not budget so strictly. We no longer had to work together. The children, to this day, resent the fact that he used money as a means of control. It was so automatic in him that I often wondered if he grew up that way," she added.

"It is no wonder that, even today, I am not impressed by anyone's bank account. My attitude towards money is that I need enough to be comfortable and safe, to be independent, and to be able to help my children in a crisis. I do not want to be controlled by money. I have no desire to be rich and do not look for it in my friends. Money can corrupt a relationship," according to Mary Jo.

Which brings Mary Jo to the last item on the list— POWER. It does seem to her that money or riches and power go together and lead to corruption. "Our society values the rich men or women and looks down on the struggling or poor. Those in authority get caught up in ordering people around. They are used to being obeyed and start to believe they have rights that others do not. I saw this with doctors and RNs when I was a student. I saw it with teachers when my children were in school. When I entered the working world after the divorce, I saw it in some of my bosses. Because I was married to a prominent business man who was well known and respected in the community, people assumed that I was well off financially. While some bosses were condescending to their employees, I never had to deal with that as they considered me an equal. I never told them otherwise."

As far as Mary Jo is concerned, sex, money, and power can be a blessing or a vice depending on how one handles them. She believes that any wife or husband who has power over their spouse diminishes the very person they vowed to love, which results in an unhappy union. "My husband did try to control me with money. In truth, he did, but it was in my need to please him and make him love me that I gave him that power."

Mary Jo's final comments on this topic: "This was a hard chapter to write. While I have to admit that I like sex, and I like having enough money to be comfortable, and I like the power of being in charge, I can see how it tends to make a person feel superior to those closest to you. I am a romantic and believe strongly that without love these gifts are nothing more than steps to arrogance. When all three of these (sex-money-power) are used to control others, to manipulate others, it reduces each one to a vice. They can be true gifts when tempered with LOVE and RESPECT."

From here to the end of this chapter, this is Nadine speaking. In reference to the introduction, many people experience satisfying sex into their very old years. I don't happen to be one of them, but I'm okay with that. Although I do remember times that it was quite enjoyable, I do not, and have not missed it for many years.

Within the framework of my marriage, money was always an issue. The prevailing belief was that there just wasn't enough. My observation was that poor management was the problem. I distinctly remember one day when I told a friend I could not join her for lunch because I didn't have $5.00, and that very evening my husband came home from work reporting that he had just purchased a new set of golf clubs for $150.00, saying it was too good a deal to pass up. Money was one of those areas that was vastly improved following the divorce even though I received nothing in terms of a one-time payment or ongoing spousal support.

Generally speaking, Social Security has been a culture changer in the United States. What started out to be a very modest supplement to incomes has become the entire source of income for many people. I myself waited to take my Social Security until I was 70 years old in an effort to maximize the amount, because I knew it would be the main source of my retirement income. I have a small pension from working at the Pleasanton Unified School District and another somewhat larger pension from working for the Veterans' Administration of the Federal Government. I worked for each of them about 12 years so my annuities are nothing close to what they would be for a lifelong employee. However, the total of these three sources leaves me with a livable income for which I am extremely grateful. It made retirement possible for me.

Power over others, with the exception of my children when they were young, is never something to which I aspired, but it's very definitely important to many, many human beings as I've observed in my lifetime. Part of my power education occurred when I was working as an administrative assistant in a high school. One of my responsibilities was assigning and managing the maintenance of the lockers. When I was new to the job I told the custodian who changed the combinations that I would need them done by a certain time in order to have the assignments made before school started. Oh, no. He made it very clear to me that they would be done when he got them done. He was in charge of what and when anything happened with lockers. From then on I was sure to ask for his timeline and work around it. Another example was when I was first hired by the VA I spoke on the telephone to a woman in Human Resources saying something like, "I was told I have the job." She interrupted me saying, "You don't have the job until I tell you, you have the job."

So, wherever we humans reside in the pecking order, we need to show others the extent of our power. Witness the incidents of abuse of various kinds. That's nothing more than power. Do what I say. I'm in charge here. I feel very fortunate that I have always been content to let someone else be in charge (Do you suppose that's a product of being the youngest of three girls?) except when it came to rearing my children. That was my job and no one else's. The power that is most important to me now is the power I have over my own life; my time, my activities, my money. I am very grateful that at this age I still have a great deal of it. High five to power!

Chapter Six
Spirituality/Faith/Religion

"Live simply, love generously, care deeply, speak kindly and leave the rest to God."

Ronald Reagan

I, Mary Jo, begin this chapter. The three topics of this chapter are so intertwined; it is puzzling to me where to begin. Let me start with my concept of spirituality. It seems to be basic within our nature. Children are comfortable with spirituality. Simplicity comes to mind. To believe in someone greater than self is a great need in everyone. It explains so many religions. I do believe that faith is a gift from God and given to everyone. To accept the gift is our individual choice. It is a lost gift if we don't nurture it, and it is up to each of us to find the path to the means of nurture. Some find it within self and in union with nature. Many find it within a church and with others. I believe that each church has a special gift and together, they form the Body of Christ. See what I mean? I cannot separate them. So it helps to hear what the others have to say.

Nadine begins. Her first religious experiences were in the Methodist Episcopal Church's Sunday School. She was particularly drawn to the stories she heard via the felt boards; Jonah and the Whale, Noah and the Ark, and the Nativity every Christmas. She has no memory of any of this information being discussed at home, nor of her parents being a part of any church activities other than occasionally her mother attending a church service. "When I started dating a Catholic boy in high school," Nadine says, "my parents became animated with their complaints regarding this relationship. My response was, 'Don't worry. I'm not going to marry him.' Oops." We all laughed. Oops was common in all our lives.

Nadine's parents took her to the local minister and the president of the local protestant college to be told of the dark side of the Catholic Church and all the reasons that she should stay away from it. "I remember most of what I was told by them and would agree with some of that now, but at the time I wanted to be the same religion as the man I married," she says. One of the first rubs came when Nadine's oldest son, about the fourth grade, brought home the Baltimore Catechism and told her she was to help him study it. She opened the book and read the first line: "How do we know that the Catholic Church is the one true church?" Her response to him was: "Well, for openers we don't know that. And I quickly determined that I should not be the one working with my children on this catechism and told his teacher just that."

Having said that, Nadine was still very comfortable within the Catholic family. She attended Mass every Sunday and all the days of obligation. Her social life was almost exclusively within the Catholic community. As noted at the beginning of "On Being Old" the friendship of this threesome was as a result of attending a Cursillo, a weekend retreat called a "short course in Christianity" as presented by the Catholic Church. Her six children were all baptized in the Catholic Church and attended Catholic schools until the family moved out of state and access to the schools was not as available. With this move came many changes: children in public schools, friendships through children's activities rather than church, introduction to alternative ways of thinking, i.e., astrology, past life regression, psychic centers, and no longer attendance at the Catholic Church, not even on Sundays.

After the divorce Nadine began attending the Unity Church which seemed to be overflowing with former Catholics. The attraction for her was the emphasis on the Love of God (as opposed to the Fear of God) and the almost total lack of rules. The Unity Church is a big proponent of metaphysical understanding (the symbolism associated with the Bible and all life stories) and A Course in Miracles. "I began reading the metaphysical teachers like Emmet Fox and Joel Goldsmith and loved the metaphysical Bible studies. I have come to the place that I believe the Bible was never intended to be a history book or to be taken literally. The metaphysical interpretations make much more sense to me," states Nadine.

"My first experience with A Course in Miracles was cursory at best but left me with a prayer for each and every occasion: 'This holy instant I give to you. You be in charge and I will follow, certain your direction gives me peace. If I need a word it is there. If I need a thought it is there. If I need but stillness and an open mind, that is there too. You are in charge at my request.' This is actually a paraphrase of the final five lessons of the 365 lessons in the course. Without my paying much attention, the act of reciting this prayer, and meaning what I said, made changes in my thinking and attitudes. I have since gone through the course another time, including a workbook which helped a great deal in understanding, and more recently a book entitled, *A Course in Miracles Made Easy*. The course is written very similarly to the Bible so, for me, needs clarification."

Nadine continues: "An interesting aside is that A Course in Miracles dovetailed with my practice as a mental health therapist in such a way that one fed and embellished the other. They were both teaching and practicing the same thing. I loved it. A basic tenant is that what we think is the most important thing, because what we think determines what we feel, which in turn determines how we behave. That is the essence of Cognitive Behavioral Theory. I had many pictures and sayings on display in my office and my favorite one said: 'Don't Believe Everything You Think.'

"So, at the present time I do not think of myself as religious, that is I don't belong to or espouse a specific belief system, but I most definitely think of myself as a spiritual being. My life now is very relaxed and calm and comfortable. I have few instances of upset or agitation and many instances of delight. It's hard to put into words, but I am content almost always with occasional instances of sheer joy," concludes Nadine.

Sam's turn to speak on the topic of spirituality/ faith/ religion: She has had "religion" since the day she was born! Her uncle (and Godfather) was an Episcopal priest. He baptized her. Her grandmother read the bible throughout twenty-seven times and was a huge influence in Sam's life. Her folks made sure she got to church every Sunday. Sam had perfect attendance at Sunday school, sang in the children's choir, continued on with the adult choir, and went to church camp every summer. When she was in high school she went to Young Life Camp, traveling on the train from St. Paul to Colorado Springs, where she conscientiously invited Christ into her life, becoming what she believed, in every sense of the word, is a "born again" Christian.

After Sam graduated from high school, her fiancé, who was Roman Catholic, was willing to convert for her, but asked if she would consider attending classes at the Cathedral of St. Paul to see what he would be giving up. "After six months of instructions I decided our religions weren't all that different, so I was re-baptized, made my first communion, and got confirmed (again!). During that six-month period I also got pregnant, and we were married in that beautiful Cathedral in St. Paul, Minnesota. I knew I wanted to have a one religion family where we could raise our children in one faith. So it all worked out for the good," exclaimed Sam.

Sam and her husband continued the tradition of being active Catholics, raising their kids with church every Sunday and CCD (Confraternity of Christian Doctrine) classes during the week. Their children even got involved in Christian youth programs in high school. Sam and her spouse were then introduced to the Cursillo, a movement in the Catholic Church with the objective to Christianize our environments, starting with themselves. They spent many years as leaders in that movement. "It was also the place where I met these two wonderful co-authors forty years ago! What a blessing it has been to reunite and share our stories!" says Sam.

She continues, "So, after all of that history, here I am in my senior years not participating much in any organized religion. Go figure! Religion, I believe, I have. Faith, however, seems to have drifted in and out of my life over the years. I have learned that I could question my religion without endangering my faith. But what has made my faith so questionable? My faith, ergo spirituality, seems to have bounced around a lot over my whole adulthood. I was taught that if I was a good Christian, there were certain expectations required. When I didn't produce those 'godly virtues' I often felt like a failure and consequently questioned my faith."

Sam goes on with her questioning: "According to our bible, God said all we have to do is profess that He is our Lord and Savior and we'll be welcomed into His kingdom. But as Christians there are always these little contingencies that say, 'if you do this, then you have to do that.' There's always more required. So, is the whole point to just keep trying and failing over and over? It's hard work! It has to entail certain practices: prayer, meditation, study, good works, sacrifice, forgiveness, humility, and above all—love. If, in fact, it is done in love, all the rules wouldn't be necessary. All of which should be done without letting guilt into the picture! Is THAT even possible?"

Sam's favorite verse in the bible has always been Philippians 4:13, "I can do all things through Christ who strengthens me." How comforting is that? However, she feels that she fails time and time again. One of the things she most likes about the Catholic Church is that you can go to Mass anywhere on earth and it would be the same mass and receive communion every day. As an Episcopalian communion was only offered once a month and she shared that she wanted it more often. If Mass is where you're fulfilled that is great. "I know we should go to church, to be part of God's community and uplift our fellow Christians. But, unfortunately, I don't feel uplifted or fulfilled from that experience, or wonder if I ever really did feel that way," she says.

"Interestingly enough, I receive those emotions in God's everyday wonders. Most especially through the five senses He has given us: sight, hearing, smell, taste, and touch. They allow us to understand and perceive the world that God created for us. That's where I see Him, that's where I feel Him, that's where I can praise and thank

Him. I think, sometimes we try to understand too much about God and forget that faith is a very intangible thing. When we say 'rest in the Lord,' I need to remember that! All I know is when I have peace and contentment it's when I'm holding one of my babies: my kids when they were little, my grandkids, and now my great grandkids, and oh, also my dogs," concludes Sam.

With all that said I, Mary Jo, now continue with my thoughts. To be spiritual, we accept that there has to be something greater than us. To see the human body and all its workings or to see nature, the seasons, the growth of seeds into plants, flowers, trees, then see them die or go dormant, and rise again during another season. Who of us is wise enough to create life in all forms? God means different things according to the different cultures. Just as I believe we must respect one another, I believe we must respect different approaches to God.

God is my spiritual father, and I take all my concerns and love to Him. Perhaps it is a result of need; nevertheless, it is mine to hold dear. His Son, Jesus, is my Lord. He guides me, saves me from myself often, listens to me, heals me, loves me, and is my companion in life. He is more than a friend, he is my brother for we share the same Father.

As I said before, faith is our precious gift from the Father. We can accept it or reject it. To believe is to have faith. Are we capable of forgiving others or even ourselves with our own ability? Look around at the state of our country and know that, just as individuals, society cannot and blames one another for our own sins, and love turns to hate.

I struggle a bit with organized religion. It seems it has gotten lost due to raising money, building bigger and better buildings, and trying to maintain peace with the powers of government. Sometimes simplicity is needed. We need to go back to what churches or religion was formed to be. It started as a comfort or strength to people who were persecuted. The need for social interaction and belief was vital for survival. It has gotten lost in the need for money. It has become a means of control over its members. I am a Catholic, and while I cherish the seven Sacraments and believe they serve every need of man and woman, the church has too much control and lays guilt on anyone who breaks one of its rules. As far as I know, which is limited knowledge; it could apply to all churches.

I still go to Mass faithfully because of the social need for friends who share my faith, to hear the Gospel, to sing songs of praise that lift my soul, to celebrate the Last Supper, and to be fed the Word of God. We are blessed in our parish at the present time with a priest who gives a short but spirit-filled sermon. Without church, I grow lax, forget to pray, rarely read Scripture, and fail to live as a true Christian. So Church, with all its faults, is a need for me. It nurtures my need for friends, for community, for knowledge, and for guidance.

Spirituality, faith, and religion are all One to me. I need all three and thank the Father for all three.

My statement on spirituality/faith/religion was written before the Corona virus and the order to shelter in place. Since then, all churches have been closed. This hit at the highest time in the Christian world, Lent & Easter. As I celebrated Easter alone (with the phone calls from my children and my niece) it was a day of reflection. As I said before, church is my support, my food, and meets my social needs. I miss it, and I miss my friends. We would go out for breakfast after Mass, but now the churches and the restaurants are closed. While I miss the social aspect of my life, there is comfort and peace while at home alone. It is a time to be grateful for all my blessings, family, and a home with warmth, lights, and running water. I have access to food and medicine. We have all slowed down, and those that I have talked to are at peace, while occasionally lonely. Some are actually enjoying the lack of hurrying here and there. It is time to embrace our basic value—needs met and family. I find that I don't need church for faith or a personal relationship with Christ. I like it for the support and for the food for thought. We get caught up in the worldly needs and don't spend time nurturing our souls. This time has slowed the world down and many have read, prayed, and looked within. I know that I have. One of the quotes that seems to fit the present time is "Maturity is the ability to think, speak and act your feelings within the bounds of dignity. The measure of your maturity is how spiritual you become during the midst of your frustration," by Samuel Ullman.

While all three of us were very spiritual in the past, this experience of sheltering in place may have deepened our convictions or our ability to look within ourselves and touch base with our souls. God brings good from all things to those who believe. My peace within comes from past experiences and learning the hard way (by trial and error) that gratitude for what we have lifts us up beyond the negatives of the world. Another way of saying it is... count your blessings!

Chapter Seven
Death of Ourselves and Others

"Death is not the opposite of life, but a part of it."
Haruki Murakami

There are some things, as they say, we can always count on, death and taxes. As young people we seldom think of either. But as we grow older it seems they both take precedence in our lives. We aren't going to talk about taxes, but the three of us have a few things to share about how we refer to death, or, the end of life, our demise, our passing, the grim reaper, the Pale Horse, the big sleep, the deceased, our expiration, the quietus, our termination, extinction, or, when the Catholic church is called in, extreme unction/last rights. Those are all terms people use, but the reality of it is that as we grow old we become increasingly aware of our mortality.

As we write this book, our planet is in the throes of the Covid-19 pandemic, making death an even bigger reality due to the constraints that governments around the world are putting on their citizens and the fear associated with it. At this time there is no cure nor is there a vaccine, so precautions are necessary. So, it is with sadness that we delve into the thoughts of death as to how it has, and how it does now, affect us. I am Sam and the presenter of this chapter.

Nadine says she doesn't spend a lot of time thinking about or worrying about her own death, but there was a time when she was terrified of the prospect. Her solution was to go to work for hospice, first as a volunteer and later as a social worker. Her theory was that if she could see what it looked like and how other people do it, she could relax. She thinks it worked. She was only present at the actual time of passing with a couple of patients and observed that both of those were very peaceful. She also saw lots and lots of the "getting ready" time. Of course, people are individuals and do things in their own way but within the differences is a similarity. According to Elizabeth Kubler-Ross, a noted authority on death and dying, the process includes denial, anger, bargaining, depression, and acceptance, not necessarily in that order nor all inclusive. The goal is to actually get to the acceptance part. Nadine saw all of that and only hopes that when it is her turn she will be at the acceptance level sooner rather than later.

Equally as hard as contemplating her own death, she says, is getting to the acceptance place when the death is of a friend or relative. The same steps apply. Grief can be debilitating. Working through it requires just that; working through it. Unresolved grief can affect all kinds of aspects of our lives without letting us know what's happening. Unresolved grief is responsible for sending many, many people to a therapist. In fact, Nadine ventured to say that the vast majority of therapy sessions could be avoided if grief were acknowledged, addressed, and reconciled. (Keep in mind that grief is not just about losing someone to death, but includes the loss of someone who is still living by divorce or geographical separation or some other way, or losing something of emotional value, or a source of income, or a bodily function, or a myriad of things that have become important to us in one way or another and are no longer available to us.)

The practical side is that when we lose someone who is important in our lives we need to fill the resulting hole with something. The goal would be to fill it with something positive, perhaps another person or a new hobby or maybe even an adventure. Nadine said that after her divorce and after enough time had passed that she could think again, she decided to go back to school and finish the education she had always wanted but for which she could never find the time and money together in the same place. As she learned in the resulting psychology courses, this is an example of sublimation, channeling into acceptable activities, considered one of the positive coping mechanisms. As she exclaimed, "Yay for me!!!"

"However," Nadine shares, "as I get older the losses come more and more frequently, and I become more and more callous to them. The losses are not felt as intensely and my reaction to them is much more philosophical; nobody gets out of this alive." To date she has lost both parents, one sister, two former boyfriends, and 10 close girlfriends, six of them dating back to high school and earlier. The first girlfriend she lost was back in 1975. She was only 35 years old and was killed in an automobile accident. Nadine said she dreamt about her friend every night for almost a year. She would wake up in the morning sure that she had actually spent the night with her. The most recent was a former boyfriend going back to her junior high days. As a comparison, she says she thinks of him only occasionally. He was 79 years old.

Just recently Nadine was informed that a former brother-in-law, with whom she has remained close, experienced a minor stroke. He appears to be very lucky and has no noticeable deficits as a result. This event followed her former husband being diagnosed with prostate cancer and now appearing to be doing very well also. Her reaction to these two possible deaths was a deep sadness, disproportionate to the events, because she said, "It brings my thoughts to the fact that me and those in my generation are very definitely the next in line for death. It is not 'if,' it's 'when.' Sobering to be sure."

Actually, she ponders, "My biggest question at this point in my life is: What happens after death? It's very bothersome to me that no one has come back to let us know. I say that as a person who has experienced very realistic past life regression which would presuppose that I would be expecting to go into yet another life following this one. That is certainly one of the possibilities as I see it. But I'm not at all convinced that it's the only one. There are so many questions and so few actual answers.

Lots of speculation. For some reason life and death as we know them are surrounded by insurmountable mystery."

Mary Jo begins: "As a nurse, I have never been a stranger to death. It is simply a process of living to our end. It is a natural part of life. It wasn't until I was in my 30s that I experienced losing two close friends, and it became more personal. MY friends left families of young children, and the loss was life changing for them. The sadness was mine also, and I missed them terribly. The loss was tempered by my belief that I would see them again in heaven."

As the years passed, Mary Jo lost more and more friends and again took comfort in her belief that it was a temporary loss. Then, her parents died followed by the loss of her older brother and younger sister. "It was hitting me in my daily life, and I mourned the loss so much that it was a physical pain. Again, my only comfort was my belief in eternal life. Each loss left me with treasured memories, and I refuse to believe that it all ends with death. We will be united again in Heaven," states Mary Jo emphatically.

"So, in my twilight years, I am face to face with my own mortality. No matter what we know to be a fact, most people do not believe that they really will die. My head knows it, but my heart believes I will live forever. When my father was facing his own death I asked him if he was afraid, and he said, 'No. I fear the process but not death itself,' and I share that feeling," she continued. There was a year in Mary Jo's life that she had such terrible pain and no relief available. It was at the end of that year that she was ready to die; just to be rid of that pain and the loss of independence. "Life, as I knew it, was over and I could not go on. Long story short, I received the help needed, healed an infection, had surgery, and was given another chance at life and independence. My gratitude was and is, totally great."

But now the body parts are starting to give out, and Mary Jo is faced with another surgery. At this age, surgery is a risk. "Am I ready to face my own death? Am I brave enough and my faith strong enough, as it was for others who faced their own deaths? It's easy to say 'yes' but the truth is until tested, we really don't know the answer. I pray that I am. I have had a wonderful life, so full of people that I have loved and who have loved me," Mary Jo stated.

Now, as life moves into a new phase, Mary Jo hangs onto the friendships that are remaining. "Am I ready to die? I have loved my life, and I love my life now. I am grateful for all the blessings I still have. Do I want to leave this life? 'No.' I treasure this life. The only thing that would make me say 'yes' is knowing that I will be reunited with people I have loved. I will go to Heaven and join my family and friends. This belief makes leaving this world less painful. My children and grandchildren are grown now and, while they will mourn, their lives are full and they will go on living. The love of family and faith in a Heavenly Father makes facing death easier," concludes Mary Jo.

The three of us, Nadine the philosopher, Mary Jo the spiritualist, and me, as Nadine calls me the true Capricorn (the doer), come at you, the reader from such different angles (and I hope you've been able to distinguish those differences throughout your reading). But here I go from much of the practical side of things!

I have not specifically asked an elderly person how they feel about the prospect of death because I didn't want to stir up thoughts that they may not want to think about. But let me tell you, I've had a lot of those thoughts now that I'm reaching that vulnerable time of my life. And I want to talk about it! It's hard to start such a touchy subject, especially with a husband or children. Denial and fear come in to play with those close to us.

My husband's philosophy, when I asked him about final wishes was, "I don't care. I'll be gone and won't know what the rest of you decide." I believe the kindest thing to do for those left behind is to take care of as many funeral obligations as possible. Those who are left to mourn have enough emotional aspects to deal with the loss of losing you without the additional burden of having to make lasting decisions.

My greatest loss, of course, has been family members. Almost all of my family lived nine hundred miles away, "back home" where I was raised. Fortunately, I was able to be there, and hold the hands of my father, mother, and my only sister when each of them were taking their last breaths. They didn't seem to be in any pain at that point, and I appreciated that as well as the peace that I felt knowing they were no longer struggling to hang on. It did not alleviate the emotional pain that I had knowing I would never see them again. Never be able to go to them for advice. Never share all the future happy AND sad occasions that would come. Never again tell them "I love you." I have also lost two brothers, but have a third brother left who is ten years older than me and will probably outlive me! But I am now the matriarch of the family and sure don't feel up to handling that position! I have learned, however, that time does really heal most wounds. We get to the place where the hurt subsides somewhat and the memories begin to flourish. Memories of a life lived kick into high gear as we age. Walt Whitman was a journalist, a baseball fan and most famously a poet who wrote in his mid-19th-century iconic collection "Leaves of Grass":

MEMORIES
How sweet the silent backward tracings!
The wanderings as in dreams—
the meditation of old times resumed
Their loves, joys, persons, voyages.
How true this rings...

(Which, as a side thought, I'm so grateful that we've created an abundance of memories with our children and grandchildren. Now we're hoping to live long enough to create some memories with the great grandchildren!)

The most traumatic death I've had to deal with was my best friend when we were both twenty-two years old. She was an only child who died in her sleep of a pulmonary embolism, leaving a husband, son and two very broken-hearted parents. Even though I was a practicing Christian since I was a little girl, she was with me when I became a born-again Christian as juniors in high school when we attended a Young Life camp in Colorado. We shared many hours reading our bibles together and many hours with our music, her on the piano and me singing and dancing! Her death left me with vivid dreams for nearly a year. Her favorite verse in the Bible was "For to me, to live is Christ, and to die is gain" (Phil. 1:21) That verse was used throughout her funeral in two services; the Christian church and the Greek Orthodox church, as her family was from the Ukraine. It was a comfort knowing she was with God. I felt it was important to empathize with her parents and support them in their grief. I always believed that "Blessings are multiplied and sorrows divided when shared with one another." But all we did was hug and cry whenever we were together! We didn't spend any time on the blessings and the sorrows weren't divided much as we all felt such pain.

I haven't given much thought as to what I would do or how I would live if I knew when I was going to die. I'm more at peace not thinking about it!! I guess I'd figure that out if it were an option to know when and/or where and/or how. Organizer that I am, however, I have already taken care of the final arrangements in order to make things easier for my family.

I don't have a "bucket list" because I'm realistic enough to know I probably couldn't cross off many items for one reason or another. It takes money to do the many things I've always wanted to do. And, as the body ages, I'm less capable and less likely to carry off those things as I grow older. I've slowed down considerably and lack the needed stamina!

I hesitate to talk about how my large, immediate family has not had to endure a loss. As a baseball person, I liken it to not talking about a pitcher throwing a no-hitter. When you mention it, the other team invariably gets a hit. Superstition is something we laugh about until it happens. There again, as far as my family goes, if I don't think about it I don't have to deal with it. We can bury our heads in the sand or live in denial. I'd like to think I'm more logical than that, but who knows?

Am I ready for death? Am I right with God? Are all my ducks in a row? Do the people I love know, without a doubt, that I love them? What happens if none of the above has been taken care of? Will I still get to see my twenty-two-year-old best friend again? Or my parents and siblings? Will anyone left behind remember me the way that I remember all who have gone before me? Our brain has the capacity to comprehend everything. Unfortunately we can't use all of it (they say we only use 10%) so we're denied the ability to seek so many answers. I often ask why that is. I guess, faith is what brings us to a peaceful understanding, but boy will I ever have questions at the pearly gates. Knowing we're going to die is a given. But not knowing the "when" or the "how" or even what happens afterward makes us a little skittish. As Nadine mentioned, "No one, absolutely no one, has come back to let us know! For some reason life and death, as we know them, are surrounded by insurmountable mystery." What a bummer!

We'd sure like to have answers! God seems to be the ultimate go-to-guy for things we don't understand or have a hard time accepting. Why would He allow such rampant pain, suffering, and death? I don't believe He does. I also refuse to believe that Satan has a hand in so many of our evil dealings. We've been given free will, thereby making us very capable of initiating every destructive thing that happens to us. God's heart must ache as He watches the suffering we inflict upon His children.

Man has been hellbent on wickedness since the beginning of time. Just refer back to Chapter Five and reflect on how sex, power, and money has caused humanity to engage in wars, death, and unspeakable sorrow and suffering.

The finality of death, when it happens quickly, or after a lingering illness is, in itself, somewhat of a blessing for that individual. It may not be as traumatic as the process leading up to it such as knowing you're dying, waiting for it to happen, and wondering how you'll feel when it does.

But for those of us left behind, however, it can be hell and can encompass navigation through so many emotions. When losing someone it is our loss, not theirs. The sadness is also ours, as is the grief. We've all heard the necessary stages of death and dying that Nadine spoke about that loved ones should experience. Hopefully we get through all of them.

The finality of death, even of those we're not close to, should, for most of us, catapult us into the acceptance stage because there is absolutely nothing we can do to change it once it has happened. So then we're left with all the normal questions of "how" and "when" because wanting those answers somehow helps us calibrate how close we are to death ourselves. Are we dealing with the same afflictions? Are we about their age? Are our lifestyles similar? But the "why" is unanswerable in most cases. Our need to know "why," especially of those we love, can plague and mystify us for a long time when we think there has got to be a reason, and we have no recourse to find out.

In the death of a young person or infant we want to blame someone or something. Humans should live a full lifetime and die of old age! Right? As Christians we turn to God for answers and all we're left with again is "acceptance."

Our bodies are typically bred to last only so long if we are fortunate enough to escape an early death. What happens after we're gone is the proverbial question! We just don't know! Our faith gives us hope of an afterlife if we choose to believe that Jesus died to make a place for us in heaven. That promise helps us look at death without the fear of dying, hopefully.

The three of us have lived long enough to have experienced many deaths of family and friends. We all have a slightly different perspective of death even though we're at that place in our lives where time is slipping away. I pray that we all go in peace.

Chapter Eight
Philosophy of Life

"Life is a sexually transmitted, terminal disease."
Oscar Wilde

Here we are at the final chapter in *On Being Old*. It just seemed important that each of us speak to our own belief system. If you have not yet come to this conclusion, it will now become obvious that we are three different people with three different and distinct approaches to life. Hopefully, the take away for each of you is that there is not one way to live, to be happy and thrive. We each have pluses and minuses. Some of them overlap and some of them are unique. Some of our philosophies are formal and can be articulated, and some of them are unwritten and buried deeply so more difficult to enunciate.

Mary Jo's Philosophy of Life

The purpose for which we decided to write this book was to share our individual lives and growth along the path to old age. And to accept all aspects of aging that we are now living through. It is not a time for lectures or psychology lessons, just a personal journey of life. To stay in our intellect is of no interest to others. There are better psychology books to read. To be honest with ourselves and others has more interest. For example, the chapter on how we dealt with indifference in a marriage or how we dealt with infidelity or a lack of love in a marriage. What was our relationships with friends, casual or close? What was our relationships with our children and what is it now? All of these issues we each have tried to share with you. Living life to the fullest isn't a question of how smart or superior we are in intellectual matters, but how honest we can be about ourselves, our goals, our achievements, our failures, and the need to maintain humility. To think we are somehow smarter or superior makes us only annoying. My philosophy is simple but not easy to live out, and it isn't mine, just adopted by me. "Know thyself"—by Plato and "Do unto others what you would have them do to you" (Matthew 7:12, Bible).

In writing this book, we hope to share our journeys and how we coped along the way. Individual development is much the same as the growth of a nation. All nature matures in stages. Dependence on others, belief in self, acceptance of strengths and weaknesses, and finally, humility and love in a mature form. Look at our nation right now. It has evolved into hate and intolerance of anyone that thinks differently. We have to grow beyond that mentality. We are all products of our history, our genes, and our experiences. Did we learn from them? Did we grow and mature? Are we now more humble, and give credit to our Creator, who gave us life and guided us through life? Or have we become our own god?

My greatest gifts are sensitivity and intuition. When used for others, they are a precious gift. When turned inward, they are a weakness. It is only when you know yourself with an honest appraisal that you can accept yourself and others. I must confess at this point that as I grow older, I grow more intolerant of people who are not true to self. There are those people who keep up appearances at all costs. At my age, I have learned to not judge but to avoid them. Old age makes me value true friends. Energy is limited, so save it for those who give life.

And that brings me to humor. It is a gift to sit with friends and laugh. Humor takes the sting out of our limitations. To realize that we aren't alone, all who have the privilege of aging must learn to see the humor in our lives and those around us. I love the friends who laugh with me. They add joy to my life. To accept our own humanity makes it possible to see and accept the same in others. It is at this stage of life that we grow beyond the need to blame others for our own failures. We are all given free will and are responsible for our own choices and not those of others.

So, now that I have entered the last stages of life, old age with its physical limitations, my own belief system, my faith in God and life after death, I find that I am grateful to God for my many blessings and His guidance through this journey. As I said earlier, my philosophy was not created by me but adopted from those wiser. To treat others with respect is to love them. Kindness begets kindness. Acceptance is a basic need in us all. We have all experienced the sting of rejection. Sometimes it takes years to climb over that obstacle.

I have shared my personal story in earlier chapters. Now I have shared my philosophy—how I perceive things, my basic belief system. To love God and be grateful for life. To make good choices in life or to be brave enough to change bad choices. To grow, to develop, to love myself so I can truly love and accept others. To realize that evil is a true force, within us and without. We are to hate the evil but love the person. None of this comes easily but slowly and with experience and old age. As we accept our limitations and believe in something greater than ourselves, we are free to embrace life as a gift. In reflecting on what I believe, I do realize that my thoughts have evolved with age and experience. While I was in bed not knowing if the pain would ever end, I read a book, *The Magic*, by Rhona Byrne and spent that time doing the exercises in each chapter. It focused on gratitude for all things, large and small, and it has given me a power over my limitations, my attitude, and was life changing.

Sam's Philosophy of Life

We don't come into this world with a predetermined philosophy of life (or, maybe we do! Who knows?) But whatever we come up with is greatly determined by our parents, environment, education, associations, and, for many of us, religion. Our philosophies are as diverse as each of us and uniquely specific as well.

Most of us don't even give thought to what our philosophy of life might be. And then, BAM, we decide to write a book and include in it a chapter so entitled! Now I have to try to put into words what I've been trying to live, consciously and/or unconsciously! We go through life filling our time with distractions and don't ask if they are important or if we find them of value. We just keep plugging along, being influenced by everyone and everything around us. But I do know one thing, "even if you're on the right track, you'll get run over if you just sit there."

It is a short time between birth and death and for most of us we don't develop a conscious "philosophy" until much later in life after we've experienced enough life to put together a reasonable, cognitive, semblance of what we think we believe to be true. Which is really only true to us alone!

In a typical American female's lifespan of 81.4 years (UNDP 2018) the changes (and adjustments) are overwhelming, especially in this day and age. Life is really just one adjustment after another! Learning to maneuver through them and survive them is each person's burden to bare and has a great deal to do with our mental attitude. Things are always changing in all areas of our existence and we can "get on the train" or "get off the track." The tools were given to us, we just have to figure out what to do with them in order to successfully make it to "old age."

I believe our purpose on earth is to procreate, to keep our species alive on this planet, along with every other living thing, or we'll cease to exist. Hopefully, by the time we've filled the earth, we'll have conquered other planets to inhabit. At any rate, while we are here it's important to realize that we have a limited time to accomplish our personal growth which is influenced by the physical, spiritual, mental, social, emotional, intellectual, environmental and occupational experiences we have. A "good" life is the objective.

Family is a key to a good life. Cultivating a good "family" has left people who are smarter than me stymied for ages. What has worked in our family, and I'm speaking as far as raising children, is everything was pretty much trial and error without any real premeditation or discussion! As near as I can figure, the things we've done right are loving them, keeping them busy, teaching them right from wrong, and being there for them. Those are very broad aspects of what to do, and even parents who do those things have no guarantees. We certainly "lucked out"!

"Do unto others as you would have them do unto you." Matthew 7:12 is the best philosophy I've ever heard of by which to live. Learning right from wrong needs to be taught at a very early age and developed through loving parents/teachers. Formal religion plays a tremendous part in our lives. A sound moral judgment is generally shaped by being exposed to good, positive, and healthy experiences, often originally nurtured through religious teachings. Even if you choose not to follow a formal religion in life, at least you've built a solid foundation with some structure and direction to understand how the world works and how to navigate in it. Time flies and we are the pilots. It's never too late to try to live up to our own expectations!

As my family grew in numbers, and my grandkids grew in age, I realized the importance of keeping in contact with them. So I broke down and joined the tech world and purchased my first cell phone at the age of 73. I send a group text every Sunday that is mostly inspirational, with helpful messages that always end with "I love you" and "have a safe week." I don't get a response from all of them every week, but I hear back from many of them and they all know that I am still here and in their corner. As families disperse all over the country and world I find it the easiest way to stay in contact. That is the one positive advantage I have found in the world of social media. Linking our kids and our extended families is a valuable commodity. It has given me a sense of being remembered and maybe they all see the wealth of knowledge that years of living can provide in their lives.

I don't believe our philosophy today has changed much from the beginning of time…providing food on the table, shelter, and family is basic to our survival. Life has certainly become more challenging to acquire those things today. Doing so takes an internal set of beliefs that begins and grows according to the things we are exposed to. A "good" person would try to live that life with integrity. How many of us attain it is an ongoing process with bumps along the way that challenge our very existence.

Nadine's Philosophy of Life

In response to Oprah's question, "What do you know for sure?" I would say: (1) The sun will come up tomorrow. It will rise in the east and set in the west as it has done each and every day of my 79 years. (2) The planet on which I live, called Earth, is round. I have sailed across oceans and have never fallen off. (3) Fire is hot and ice is cold. Wind can make a howling sound coming through a canyon and the ground feels solid under my feet. Fire, water, air and earth are the elements represented by the signs of the zodiac, of which there are 12. (4) For some reason, that I don't know, 12 is a significant number in the Judeo-Christian world. There are 12 months in a year, 12 hours on the face of a clock, 12 eggs in a dozen, 12 inches in a foot, 12 people on a jury, Jesus had 12 apostles representing the 12 tribes of Israel, and according to the Book of Revelation, the kingdom of God has 12 gates guarded by 12 angels. Oh, and I walked out of my office to begin my retirement at 12:12:12 on 12/12/12. And finally, (5) people are born and people die. And there is a vast array of behaviors in between those two events which I have always found fascinating and am forever trying to understand.

Obviously there is a big difference between what I know, for sure, and what I believe. I believe we are all children of God. No one is better or worse than anyone else in terms of value as a human being. My father used to quote this saying: "There is just enough good in the worst of us, and just enough bad in the best of us, that it ill behooves any of us to find fault with the rest of us." I'm not sure that he knew or cared who had said it, and I found out via the internet that it was James Adams, Robert Louis Stevenson and Edgar Cayce; perhaps each of them paraphrasing the other.

I believe that as children of God we are all on our individual paths back to Him/Her/It. I don't believe that one path is better than another, nor that it is possible to be on a path that keeps us from getting to God. Eventually we will all get there and we've got eternity to do so. Let us all be patient with ourselves and with everyone else. Just relax and breathe.

I believe that there is only one God; i.e. Higher Power, The Force, Lord, Great Spirit, Creator, Allah, Jehovah, by whatever name It is called. And this God is not a being but an energy, a force, so probably neither Him or Her are appropriate terms of reference.

I believe the devil is not an equal but opposite force. It is simply symbolic of <u>thinking</u> we are away from God. The word Satan comes from the planet Saturn which at the time of its discovery was the furthest planet from the Sun (son). The battle between good and evil is our individual battle of either consciously acknowledging that we <u>cannot</u> separate from God or thinking we are in fact separate and on our own.

I believe that what we think might be the most important part of who we are. Cognitive Behavioral Theory says that what you think determines how you feel and consequently how you behave. A Course in Miracles emphasizes thought as our primary function, the determiner of everything, and the one thing over which we have control. I understand the following is a quote from Mahatma Gandhi. I first saw it on the door of a woman living in a halfway house for substance abuse.

(1) Keep your thoughts positive because your thoughts become your words.

(2) Keep your words positive because your words become your actions.

(3) Keep your actions positive because your actions become your habits.

(4) Keep your habits positive because your habits become your values.

(5) Keep your values positive because your values become your destiny.

I have this framed and hanging above the desk where I am now seated, typing on my computer. I also believe in Karma; "whatsoever a man soweth, that shall he also reap" (Galatians 6:7, Bible), which I see reflected in Gandhi's quotation.

I believe that I have wasted a great deal of time in this life worrying needlessly, making judgments indiscriminately, and participating in negativity. I often think of what I might have accomplished if that time had been spent more productively; not in terms of something that would be labeled successful by the world, but something that I would have experienced as spiritual growth.

I guess if I were giving out advice it would be:

(1) Know that you are never alone. If you close your eyes and go inside you can feel God's presence.

(2) Know that God wants only the best for you so allow IT to be in charge.

(3) Know that all the things you love (people, places, things, abilities) are there as guides to your path. Don't hesitate to follow them.

(4) Take advantage of every opportunity to be happy, have fun, and be joyful.

(5) Be respectful of others and yourself. (That is "loving your neighbor as yourself." Paraphrase of Matthew 22:37-39, Bible.)

Epilogue

"Three universal truths: (1) Things are going to change, (2) We need help from others, and (3) Be kind to yourself."

Ken Burns

Three seniors, oldies-but-goodies, left over from the generation of the 1950s teeny boppers, continue to live and function into the next century. They have become the matriarchs of each of their families, a title given only because of succession but accepted with gratitude. Catching up after forty years we admit we may not have it altogether, but together we have it all: faith, family, friends, and love. What more is there?

We have tried to cover the topics of our lives, some we shared, some we didn't, as the result of our monthly lunch/work sessions. With the time limit on life, and a sum total of 235 years of living that we represent, we have entered a well-needed and well-earned station in life that allows us to pause, reflect and evaluate what has transpired in our lives, and helps us truly appreciate the journey we've each made.

This is our story of how we enjoy and survive old age, hopefully with grace, humor, and countless doctors' visits. As Sam referenced in Chapter One, her doctor was notified years ago to literally help her to keep putting one foot in front of the other. Her health records can corroborate how much she believes in taking care of things that may or may not be vital. "So far, so good!" she says. Mary Jo, if you recall, was having a knee problem and has since taken care of that with a full replacement, which she sailed right through! And, after hip replacement and the inability to maneuver her body like she wanted, Nadine has gained back the mobility and stamina needed to tackle most projects. So, we have prevailed. Most certainly with determination! "Acceptance" and "gratitude" have real meaning at this stage.

Mary Jo made the comment that writing this book and looking within on every aspect of our being was enlightening. We learned how different we all are and the different paths we have taken, and there is total acceptance of those differences because we love one another. There was certainly a lot of sameness: The body aging affected us all pretty much the same, the limitations were pretty much the same, and we were able to laugh at ourselves. It was freeing to share these things with others who are walking the same path. Nadine acknowledges how extremely lucky we've been in this lifetime to not have experienced anything truly traumatic. We now have a total of fifteen adult children all of whom are fully functional, thirty-six grandchildren and ten great-grandchildren who, so far, fit into that same mold. So, we all feel truly blessed. Being women and mothers, the three of us believe we will always have the need to nurture. Therefore, between us we have five dogs to mother. What a blessing they have all become.

We began writing this book a year and a half ago, during which we shared some events that we were each looking forward to. (Please note that we all feel it is important for the older generation to have things to look forward to!) At this time, however, Nadine has had to cancel her 80th birthday party due to travel complications from the Covid-19 pandemic. The party is rescheduled for next year, but the sense of excitement and anticipation are no longer there. Sam's trip to Europe had to be cancelled for the same reason. And it was the only time in her husband's life that he was willing to fly over the "pond," something he hoped would greatly please her. Unfortunately, Mary Jo's grandson's wedding had to be cancelled and rescheduled at a later date with the possibility of a much smaller gathering. So, we've learned that things are always changing, and we need to continue to roll with the punches.

Our parents were of a generation that did not tell us much. We learned many things from observation. Growing old looked a lot easier for them from our point of view then! So, we have tried to break that element of culture by sharing more information with our kids. Our children have shown a greater capacity to communicate. And now our grandkids live in a world that chooses to text, and they have information at their fingertips per their digital devices. As did our parents, we may not have provided our children and grandchildren with maps for direction. Each generation comes in with a new set of values and options, so it may not be wise or even possible to direct them in our ways. But, hopefully, we have given them the tools they need to navigate through all the choices they're making. "If you don't know, Grandma, Google it!" That is what the kids tell us. Not all answers are on the internet, however. If you're looking for an experience-tested response, it's best to check with us old people.

It is our hope that while we are three totally different people with totally different views on most subjects, perhaps you will identify with one of the characters and find a path and companionship into yourself as we did.

GOOD AFTERNOON
AND GOD BLESS

9 798886 043594